Official Know-It-All Guide™ DISCARD

ADVANCED HYPNOTISM

Your Absolute, Quintessential,
All You Wanted to Know,
Complete Guide

Dr. Rachel Copelan

Frederick Fell Publishers, Inc.

Fell's Official Know-It-All Guide

Frederick Fell Publishers, Inc.

2131 Hollywood Boulevard, Suite 305

Hollywood, Florida 33020

954-925-5242

e-mail: fellpub@aol.com

Visit our Web site at www.fellpub.com

Interior Design: Rodrigo C. Pinto, Jimmy Navarro, Edgar Roa, and Sergio Negrette

Cover design by: Lora Horton & Carey Jacobs

Library of Congress Cataloging-in-Publication Data

Copelan, Rachel.
  Fell's official know-it-all guide : advanced hypnotism / Rachel Copelan.
    p.cm.
Includes bibliographical references.
  ISBN 0-88391-060-8 (pbk.)
1. Hypnotism--Popular works. I. Title: Advanced hypnotism. II. Title.

RC498.C67 2001
615.8'512--dc21

                        2001004333

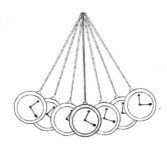

CONTENTS: ADVANCED HYPNOSIS UPDATED

INTRODUCTION

I-1

Here we are - in a new century with old century problems still clinging like tentacles of an octopus. Fortunately, there's hope. Mind to body healing is now mainstream, and hypnosis is at the cutting edge. It is now accepted within the field of psychology, that hypnosis can shorten the time of behavior modification, in dealing with addictions. This is equally true in the area of physical healing. People who use hypnosis reduce visits to doctors by 30% to 60%."

Hypnosis training is a popular part of health programs in various medical centers and teaching facilities. In the first issue of 2000, Prevention Magazine cites numerous examples of how hypnotic "energy" healing is proliferating throughout the country. In New York City, the Center for Health and Healing, a department of Beth Israel Hospital, is training patients to use hypnosis for mind-body health care. Also, at the New York Presbyterian Hospital, patients in the Heart-Assist Program are given the option of various therapies, with hypnosis leading the list.

In California, UCLA's Healthcare Newsletter announces "Hypnosis and Mind-Body Medicine to affect healing, modify physical symptoms and promote well-being."

In addition, between the East and West coast, there's Boulder, Colorado's Pain Alleviation Center. People who have tried and failed to ease pain with medication and surgery, are now getting relief the natural way, with mind-power. This is just one of many mushrooming groups, which teach hypnosis empowerment for health.

This book presents hundreds of techniques to enhance life from womb to tomb, from painless birth to vigorous old-age. In group therapy, hypnosis is the most cost effective way to correct massive problems such as: Alcohol; Drug Addiction; School violence; Dyslexia and illiteracy. With its use, we can train the unemployed. Enable the disabled. Diminish crime. Curb gang warfare. Assist prison rehab.. Diminish recidivism. Help the homeless. etc.

Millions are being spent treating sick people who should not have gotten sick in the first place. Caught up in the gusty swirl of time, most people reach the end of life without having lived in health and happiness.

Because of the enormous number of afflicted, addicted people, group hypnotherapy is the fastest, most efficient means. There are many compelling issues to be resolved. Building self-esteem for youth, will be a priority. A computer network will be used to enlighten and recruit volunteers. Individuals already trained will become counselors and mentors to others in need of help.

Hypnosis is the simplest, least expensive way for society to help millions of lost souls struggling to find their way to a better life. We need to bring hope to the hopeless and security to the insecure. Groups will gather at sites that already exist - churches, schools, community centers, union halls, or any structure with a meeting room. Hospitals are already in the vanguard of this new approach.

In the United States, one of the most advanced countries in the world, we have only one doctor for every 3,171 persons. The number of people who depend on a doctor has tripled since 1931. There's a universal need for the kind of higher consciousness that hypnosis provides. If ever a time cried out for expanded wisdom, it is now. The future of human life on this planet requires eliminating gross selfishness and replacing it with communal involvement. Change can only come when people care and share. When the richest help the poorest; when the healthy help heal the sick; when the most intelligent help the least; when the able enable the disabled.

Part One:
FOR BEGINNERS

CHAPTER 1

EARLY HUMANS USED THE TRANCE

Medicine Men, Mystics, Voodoo Magic
Hypnosis for Interplanetary Travel

Homo sapiens have been on this planet for over forty thousand years. Through all that time, in every area of the globe, some form of trance induction has taken place. Modern hypnotherapy is a natural extension of the mystical practices of our ancestors, and has been elevated to a science.

Before language was invented, humans were unaware of their ability to control events. They felt helpless because they didn't know they had a brain, with power to affect situations in their lives. They believed an all powerful, unseen force dominated them, from the outside. In early evolution, humanoids finally became humans when they realized they could think and make choices.

Fossil discoveries reveal that the brain doubled in size in the first million years, and then doubled again in the next million years. Brain-size during those crucial three million years allowed humans to develop the capacity to think for themselves.

As the human brain grew even larger, we developed cognitive thinking. This made it possible to store information in memories. Memory storage has been our means of passing information from one generation to the next, expanding knowledge to the young.

We have at our disposal today, many hypnotic methods to enhance the power of the mind. If we harness that power, we can make the world of the new century a thing of nobility beyond the dreams of ancient prophets. We have everything we need with which to build the world of our ancestor's dreams, where each individual reaches the highest peak of individual potential.

Primitives had no way of knowing what we have learned since then — Each of us has, built into our brains the machinery to enhance whatever we believe in. Modern-day hypnosis allows us to become inner directed and self protected, rather than dependent on an outside force.

Today, hypnosis has gained the respect of leading researchers and health professionals. We know now hypnosis is a science of the mind and a useful adjunct to healing in the physical as well as psychological field.

As primitive humans developed consciousness of the world around them, our ape-like ancestors became intrigued with the unknown, especially the strange behavior of the sun. This shining ball which arose in the morning and disappeared at night, brought with it fear and apprehension.

Fire, because of its link to the sun, became the catalyst for prayer, which eventually would lead to the awareness of the trance-state. Prehistoric cave paintings attest to this phenomenon. Archeologists and social scientists have provided us with additional information suggesting hypnosis existed long before the word was invented or the mechanics understood.

TRANCE, PRAYER AND HYPNOSIS

Fertility rites featuring the trance state of ecstasy, were held to increase the tribe, as well as to glorify the harvest and hunting. Men and women sought to link themselves with the unseen power, hoping for sympathetic response. This link was accomplished by not only chanting and prayers, but also sensual dancing to the beat of rustic instruments. Their interactive rhythmic movements and sound created an early form of group hypnosis. Some tribes used hallucinogenic drugs, which further deepened the trance state.

One can still witness these eerie practices in the Voodoo festivals of today's primitive people; I have seen their eyes become glassy as they tremble and breath in a staccato manner. In this altered state they are able to pierce their skin and endure tattooing without experiencing the feeling of pain.

THE PHYSICAL AND THE SPIRITUAL

Throughout time, humans have been driven by two separated needs, physical and spiritual, dividing their flesh from their spirit. Early Hindu holy-men and Yogis did recognize the connection between rhythmic breathing, and mental imagery, but didn't know the part the brain played in bringing about physical changes. Therefore they imagined a supernatural force. Today, we know that mind-healing is a power which we all possess.

Hypnotism has been practiced under numerous labels all over the world since antiquity. There are allusions to trance healing in both the Talmud and the Bible. Regardless of what it is called, the power of suggestion, coupled with belief explains many of the so-called religious and metaphysical "miracles."

Before science, our primitive ancestors imbued nature with magical meaning. The cloud formations. The rain. The stars. The moon. Thunder was a warning. Tornadoes were punishment. Each night they prayed for the return of their savior, the sun. Without light they could not hunt and feed their families. The dominant problem of survival gave birth to worship of the mystical. This has clouded people's perception of their own strength, until this day.

The trance induction was carried out by medicine men and priests, and became part of many religious practices around the world. The act of chanting and repetition of prayer brought about a state of mind, akin to hypnosis. Prayer was, and still is, subliminal suggestion. During these passionate experiences, some primitives would reach a frenzied trance. They would then pierce their faces and bodies without pain or bleeding. They already knew how to perform body catalepsy and other mentally directed feats, still being demonstrated in many parts of the world.

EARLY SIGNS OF PSYCHOSOMATIC PHENOMENA

The condition called, "stigmata", (wounds and bleeding from parts of the body) is a way of identifying with Christ's agony. Modern science tells us the mind is capable of causing this kind of changes in the body, based on emotional intensity and focused imagery. What was a mystery then is no longer a mystery. Expectation profoundly affects outcome. The practice of hypnotic phenomena is also found in the history of ancient Persian Magi, as well as in China and India.

Yoga meditation, still popular today, is a carry-over from ancient times. It works well for relaxing and rising above stress. However, if you want to eliminate problems instead of transcending them, try hypnosis. Instead of escaping bodily needs by detachment and dispassion, we are going to take you in the other direction, to confront problems and eliminate them. Let's take a look way back, before Jesus Christ was born.

HYPNOSIS - 4000 B.C. TO 2000 A.D.

As far back as 4000 B.C., Assyro-Babylonia was the center of civilization. In the ancient temples, torches burned as chanting and prayer were combined with herbal healing. The altered state of mind and natural remedies were used as primary treatment for a host of ailments. Pain was alleviated by Priests who used fire for focusing the patient's concentration.

Early cave drawings show pain alleviation by eye to eye contact, similar to the way some modern hypnotists work to anesthetize a subject before surgery. Authoritative, commands were given by the practitioner to ease the area of suffering. Gods were called upon to exorcise the evil curse of illness. This corresponds in much the way modern stage hypnotists apply authoritative commands to their subjects.

Trance states were also attained by the use of drum beats or gongs, during prayer ceremonies'. Initiation into adulthood by primitive tribes, was the most significant of all of the festivals. Early societies believed young men came under the influence of demonic powers when they reached puberty.

VIRGINS PUT IN TRANCE BEFORE SACRIFICE

Many ancient cultures perceived the female as the spiritual link to the unknown, because she was endowed with the ability to give birth. Young virgins were hypnotized and drugged before being offered as sacrificial gifts to protect tribes from the wrath of angry gods. We have ample reason to believe that hypnosis was used based on art found in ancient papyrus scrolls, cave paintings, sculptures and bas-reliefs.

Hypnosis, in some form has appeared spontaneously, all over the world, wherever human beings have gathered. We still find variations being practiced in primitive areas of the globe. Travelers through the east are familiar with the sight of Hindu Fakirs who charm snakes with the monotonous droning sound of their flutes. Sometimes the charmer mesmerizes himself. Even onlookers may drift into hypnotic stares.

2000 B.C.- EASTERN MEDITATION

Wang Tai, founder of Chinese medicine, taught medical students how to use the entranced mind to help ease a variety of ailments, both physical and emotional. In India, Hindu Veda introduced methods to focus the patient's mind on specific organs which needed healing.

1552 B.C. - LAYING ON OF HANDS

The Ebers Papyrus, an ancient document, reveals that the theory and practice of hypnosis was evident in the earlyist Egyptian medicine. The document describes a technique used by physicians of that period, in which the doctor placed his hand on the head of his patient, who then closed his eyes and concentrated on the affected part of his body. The doctor would act as a channel through which a supposedly supernatural force would heal the patient's illness. Now we know that the patient is doing his/her own healing by using guided-imagery.

928 B.C.- PAINLESS SURGERY

Literature of this period displays a Greek engraving showing Chiron, a physician of the time, placing a subject in a trance before performing surgery. The patient's induction was accomplished by chanting prayer words, which called upon the Gods to assist the surgeon, and bless the afflicted one.

Hand-passes over parts of the body were also used in combination with "aroma-therapy," which is still a popular adjunct to modern holistic therapy. The patient is told to inhale deeply while sniffing perfumes, incense or medicinal herbs. In ancient times until the present, it is always the power of suggestion that brings about the wanted results.

400 - 377 B.C THE HOLISTIC APPROACH

The famous Greek physician, Hippocrates, also used trance healing. This is the same Hippocrates whose oath, formulated 2000 years ago, is still part of the graduation ceremonies for medical students.

He believed character, personality and mental attitude was linked to the type of illness suffered. His theory was the precursor to the modern theory and practice of 'Psychosomatic Medicine.'

Hippocrates, considered the father of modern medicine said, "It is more important to know what kind of person has a disease than to know what kind of disease a person has." He has been proven to be correct. We have learned from researchers about the "cancer profile." And, in the area of heart disease, "A and B type" personality (stressed or relaxed), is linked to the degree of risk for heart attack.

Hippocrates also said,: "Afflictions suffered by the body, the soul sees with shut eyes." He recognized that with visualization, greater healing would take place.

THE POWER OF HEALING SPREADS

During the period of the rise of the great Roman Empire most of its culture was borrowed from the Greeks. This included the practice of hypnotic healing. Men of great wisdom, experts in the art of trance-induction, were imported from Greece to Rome. In the wars, the conquering army took them as slaves and forced them to teach physicians skills which had become successful in both Greece and Egypt.

Way back then, they already knew that many ailments have their origin in mental and physical stress. Today, we understand illnesses such as ulcers, headaches, and assorted other maladies are directly affected by emotional imbalance. According to a number of enlightened doctors, seventy-five percent of physical symptoms fall into this category.

300-270 B.C. EGYPTIAN SLEEP TEMPLES

King Pyrhus of Egypt, was one of many ancient Priest-Kings, who converted Houses of Worship into sites where they combined prayer with hypnotic healing. These were called "Sleep Temples" and served as a combination of church and hospital. Egyptologists have discovered numerous paintings, showing worshippers in trance. The reclining positions, posture and facial expression are identical to modern hypnotic induction.

Because of the dramatic results in rapid healing, trance induction spread throughout the world, from golden temple to darkest jungles. Bible stories attribute the natural phenomena of psychosomatic healing to supernatural forces. It was believed God, in his omnipotence, caused illness to appear as punishment, while cures were a sign of forgiveness.

1000-1700 A.D. SYMPATHETIC MAGNETISM

Hypnotic techniques, combined with magnets, were popular for centuries as a means of healing. Before astronomy gave us information about the universe, many believed magnetism emanated from celestial bodies which sent healing power into our planet. Queen Elizabeth in 1600 was treated by the royal physician in this manner. Her body was covered with magnets as she napped, which probably worked because of the placebo affect.

1734 1815 A.D. MESMER'S MASS HEALINGS

Franz Anton Mesmer, a physician at age 32, discovered he could "mesmerize" large groups of people at the same time. He believed he was invested with a gift from God. Using his charismatic power, he conducted mass ritual ceremonies which actually brought about countless healings. After basking in glory for fifteen years he was declared a quack by the medical community and put out of practice. However, we need to honor him because he was the first person to use methods of group induction, so valuable in helping reduce today's widespread problems.

1860-1890 A.D. - DEVELOPMENT OF SOMNABULISM

Jean Martin Charcot, French neurologist, found that hypnosis was linked to the central nervous system. Through suggesting he brought about physical alterations such as, lethargy, catalepsy and somnambulism (a deep level of hypnosis). This led to the differentiation of the levels of hypnotic induction, later substantiated as brain waves from Beta (awake) to Delta (sleep).
Charcot was highly regarded as a specialist in hysteria, locomotion ataxia and

asphasia. Cerebrospinal sclerosis was named Charcot's disease. He taught scientists from around the world, including the Austrian physician, Sigmund Freud. As an adventurous thinker, he also believed the tides, the earth's gravity and the positions of the stars affected the afflicted and could help heal them, while in the altered mind-state.

1872-1926 A.D. RASPUTIN'S MAGNETIC EYES

Rasputin's contribution to the history of hypnosis is mainly negative. As a confidence man, this self-styled monk was infamous for his sexual exploits in the Russian court of Tsar Nicholas II and Tsarina Alexandria. He became a Monk by joining a heretical religious sect of flagellants, who beat themselves for redemption. Rasputin led the group in rituals of self-torture. To ease their pain and stop the profuse bleeding, he used his outstanding hypnotic skills and became world famous.

The Tsarina regarded Rasputin as a saint because he was able to relieve symptoms of hemophilia in her son, and to release her own sexual inhibitions. At this time, hypnosis was seen as religious magic and the Tsarina thought of him as a gift from God. Others saw him as, "The Holy Devil." Actually, he was more of a confidence man, a master trickster who used his power to dominate the royal family. Still, he had a saving grace; he was able to help many sickly children regain health.

In a desperate attempt to remove Rasputin's influence, in 1916, Prince Felix Yusupov plotted the monk's murder with a conspiracy of noblemen, who claimed Rasputin had seduced their wives with his piercing vision and seductive voice. Yusupov added huge amounts of cyanide to Rasputin's favorite cakes, then invited Rasputin to have tea at the palace.

Despite the poisonous party, Rasputin looked the plotters in the eye and remained healthy. In disgust, the Prince shot the magic-priest and left him for dead. Instead, Rasputin rallied his hypnotic energy and rose up from the floor. Then, with inhuman strength, he attacked his assassins. Many more bullets followed, to no avail. He seemed indestructible.

Finally, Rasputin was held down by six men and castrated. His bullet-ridden, bloody body still remained alive, when tossed into a raging river. When his body was retrieved, it was discovered he had not died from the bullets or loss of blood, but drowned because he had never learned to swim.

1884 A.D. JAMES BRAID, NEURO-HYPNOSIS

James Braid, a Scottish physician, has been referred to as "The Father of Modern Hypnosis." He coined the term "Hypnosis," taking it from the Greek word meaning, sleep. The word has proved to be a misnomer. You will discover in the next chapter, that there are notable differences in brain activity during sleep and during the hypnotic trance. Braid presented a paper to the British Medical Association based on his theory that hypnosis was a form of sleep, useful to control the nervous system of patients suffering epilepsy and hysteria.

Though he was originally a follower of Mesmer, he scoffed at the idea of magical powers and developed the progressive theory that the subject's expectation added to the healing due to the individual's imagination.

1856-1939 A.D. FREUD'S HYPNO-ANALYSIS

Sigmund Freud carried hypnosis from the 19th into the 20 century. (This book is intended to carry the art from the 20th to the 21 century). Frued's discovery of psychoanalysis in the late 1800's, called attention to the connection between mental/nervous disorders and physical problems. He experimented with hypnosis and dream analysis to prove: early memories affect our sensory responses to whatever happens at the moment.

He planned to use hypnosis to develop his theory of the subconscious, but uncovered more than he anticipated — he eventually changed medical opinion about the workings of the mind and its affect upon the body.

While some of his theories relating to the Oedipus complex, have since been challenged, the work he pioneered in dream analysis has been recognized as valid by most professionals in the psychological field. When he helped an hysterically blind girl regain her sight through guided imagery while she was under deep hypnosis, his fame grew throughout the medical world, and has persisted to this day.

ALBERT ADLER, 1870-1937

As one of Freud's Austrian contemporary, Albert Adler left the orthodox psychoanalytic school to experiment with trance induction. In 1935, Adler and his family moved to the United States and was a frequent guest professor at Columbia University. In his analysis of individual development, he stressed the importance of negative and positive self-image. He is the originator of the concept of "The Inferiority Complex." This led to his work on the theory and practice of psychosomatic etiology of mental/emotional illness. He was a pioneer in the mind-to-body approach, which is now widely applied to many medical-hypnosis techniques and methodology.

1857-1926 A.D. COUE'S AUTOSUGGESTION

Emile Coue, French psychotherapist, was the grandfather of self-induced improvement. He recognized the role played by a subject's acceptance of positive suggestion. He is the forerunner of present day affirmative thinkers. He cured patients by having them repeat over and over again: "Every day in every way, I am getting better and better."

His contribution is responsible for techniques in applying autosuggestion during self-hypnosis. Positive suggestion not only plays an important part in the prevention and cure of disease, but also in the realization of one's higher potential.

1904..A.D. PAVLOV'S CONDITIONED REFFLEX

Dr. Ivan Pavlov, Russian physiologist, received the Nobel prize for his contribution in researching impulsive human behavior. His innovative work with animals led to the discovery of the conditioned reflex. Pavlov would ring a bell, then offer food to a dog. After repetitions, the dog would salivate whenever he heard the bell, even when he was not hungry. Human beings react in the same way. That is why sixty percent of Americans are overweight and forty percent have substance-dependency problems.

1955-2000 A.D. WORLDWIDE ACCEPTANCE

In 1955 the British Medical Association officially approved hypnosis for treating psycho-neuroses, anesthesia for pain relief, surgery and childbirth. Three years later, in 1958, The American Council on Mental Health of The American Medical Association followed suit.

American physicians emphasized that there are uses for hypnosis as an adjunct to medicine. They stressed proper training for hypnosis practitioners and condemned stage entertainment. William S. Kroger, Milton Erickson, Leo Wollmam, William Bryant are a few of the many AMA members who spent years promoting the usefulness of hypnosis.

Hans Selye, a physician who has been described a the father of the theory of "psychosomatic" medicine, also believed in the efficacy of mind-healing. His excellent book, "Stress of Life" explains that many ailments such as headaches, backaches, and stomach ulcers are directly attributable to stress and mental/emotional disturbances.

Other books, such as this author's "How to Hypnotize Yourself and Others," promote empowerment of the subject, rather than the obsolete notion that the hypnotist must overpower the subject. During this period, thousands of men and women, have become professional hypnotists, using new-age hypnotic techniques.

WIDE APPLICATIONS FOR THE 21st CENTURY

High level research is going on in many colleges and medical schools throughout the world. Medical doctors, dentists and surgeons are participating in worldwide conventions that draw thousands of respected professionals, who used hypnotic techniques in their practice.

We have entered a new century when we will have to draw upon all the wisdom of history to combat life endangering human behavior. Serious changes in attitudes and values are required for human survival. In the past century people were conditioned to escape reality through intoxication.

At last count, United States Health Department statistics indicated:

12 million are alcoholics;
10 million use marijuana;
61 million smoke cigarettes;
130 million crave caffeine;
1.5 million use Cocaine/crack;
800,000 Amphetamines addicts;
200,000 are dependent on heroin;
80% have stress related ailments;
60% are 10 to 50 lbs. overweight;
70% suffer from sleep disorders.
In addition to curbing and correcting the above, hypnosis can empower everyone to enhance their own lives and respect the lives of others.

PROGRESS IN THE 1900'S

While vestiges of the past still resonate today, the big difference between ancient practices and modern hypnotherapy is that today the participant is in control, rather than an outside force. Because of this difference, hypnosis has become an empowering force - mentally, emotionally, physically, and spiritually, for millions of people.

From it's primitive beginning, through centuries of superstition, hypnosis has finally become mainstream. Now, a large segment of the medical community use altered-state techniques as an adjunct to traditional methods of healing. Awareness of this fact is emerging in many areas, where it is combined with other modalities such as Nu-Age healing. It is also valuable as an adjunct to traditional medicine (Anesthesia), and psychiatry (Abreaction).

From it's primitive beginning, through centuries of mysticism, hypnosis was finally recognized in the mid 1900's, as a modern science. It has finally become mainstream as a large segment of the medical community use altered-state techniques. Once humans became aware of the power of mind-control, intelligence and creative thinking began to flourish.

Those of us who work in an holistic way to help overcome psychosomatic illness, know the brain's connection to physical responses. We know that whenever a suggestion is repeated over and over again, it becomes a conditioned reflex. The power of suggestion, coupled with faith, explains many other so-called religious and metaphysical "miracles".

Over a century ago, newspapers printed announcements of new births. One headline announced:

1890'S - PAINLESS BIRTH DURING MESMERIC TRANCE

The news spread around the world. It soon became the chic thing to do among the wealthy and aristocratic. Around the same time, at the turn of the 19th century, it was a pioneering female obstetrician, Dr. (Mme) Dobrovolsky of Switzerland, who reported a case in which a post-hypnotic suggestion of analgesia was given nine days before delivery. The pregnant woman was instructed to stroke her belly periodically and repeat the phrase, "easy birth."

Later the woman reported that the birth was almost painless. The doctor announced: "I could not have gotten a more passive condition had I used chloroform."

During the 20th century many pregnancies and deliveries were made easier with hypnotic suggestion. In my own practice I teach self-hypnosis to the expectant mother as soon as possible so that she has the skill to alleviate pain long before the actual birth.

21st CENTURY CHALLENGE: ABOLISH 5 ADDICTIONS

1. **ALCOHOL** is a psychoactive, mind-altering drug. It alters moods, and causes changes in the body and brain. Alcohol is a "downer" because it depresses the central nervous system. This can cause slurred speech, passing out, and loss of memory. In addition, the medical consequences are horrendous, everything from cancer to heart disease.

2. **MARIJUANA,** like alcohol, starts out being used as a relaxant. Some people who are uptight initially feel relaxed. However, drugs cannot give the power of happy feeling to those who are deeply disturbed. It only helps to disturb them even more. If you can feeld high with marijuana, you can feel it just as elated, naturally.

3. **CIGARETTE SMOKING...** is the most preventable cause of death and illness in the industrial world. There's evidence that cigarette smoking is responsible for more than one out of five deaths in the United States. One wonders why people who are aware of this danger continue to smoke. The answer is nicotine, a drug as addictive as heroin and cocaine. The good news is that anybody who wants to stop an do so with hypnosis. For some people quitting a pack of cigarettes a day takes just one or two hypnotic sessions.

4. **ASSORTED DRUG ADDICTIONS...** Some use drugs to "blow their minds," and sometimes lose their minds altogether, as a result. There are over 10 million Americans taking legitimate pep pills regularly. It is also estimated that between 5 and 10 million people are addicted to drugs outside the law. Both are equally harmful. Drug dependency starts early in our profit-oriented society and hardly anyone is free of its lure many users. "There is a very real danger that as little as one experience with marijuana could cause some psychotic disorder such as paranoia, withdrawal, depression, and these

disorders could linger for months or even years after the drug experience.

5. **EATING DISORDERS.** There are at least a dozen food related problems that are affected by stress and can be helped through individual or group hypnosis: Overweight. Underweight. Ulcers. norexia. Bulimia. Diet Discipline - (for conditions such as Diabetes, Cholesterol, Cancer, etc.)

Entering hypnosis not only results in better health, but also brings spiritual awareness of the most profound kind. Because of the high level of human intelligence, we are ready now to enjoy an expanded life — the sky's the limit!.

HYPNOSIS AND SPACE TRAVEL FOR EVERYONE

Beyond the mind miracles of the past, hypnosis presents many practical uses for the Space Age.

Hypnotists will be called upon to utilize their knowledge in the expanding interest in the human flight into space. This potential tool will aid our ability to survive under unusual conditions, such as loss of gravity. For the trainee, an altered state of mind will facilitate his/her adaptation to the change of atmosphere.

1... To aid the candidate, imagery will suggest that the person is undergoing an actual, rather than simulated testing. In this way, selection of participants will be more accurate.

2... Ultra deep hypnosis can be effective to reduce the metabolic rate and the amount of oxygen consumption used. Conservation of physical energy is an extra bonus.

3... Hypnosis is of inestimable use in assuring space travelers maintain unusual and uncomfortable positions for long intervals in a crowded, unnatural environment.

4... Lowering of stress related to weightlessness; cramped quarters; lack of normal exercise; the forced proximity of other people's bodies.

5... Maintaining emotional and mental equilibrium and other psychological factors such as concerns about family, job performance, homesickness and fear of the unknown.

6... Adaptive responses can be strengthened for greater acclimation to new surroundings upon landing in foreign territory, as well as the return to the earth's surface.

CHAPTER 2

GET TO KNOW YOUR AMAZING BRAIN

Hypnosis Actualizes Your Potential

Induction Into Your Trance Level

Although hypnosis was practiced long before it was understood, it is only in the past century that scientists discovered the role that the brain plays in our bodily functions and emotions responses. Now we know that the hypnotic trance-state puts us in touch with a section of the brain which is receptive to suggestion, and can be trained to increase health both mentally and physically.

This three to four pound, jelly-like substance we call "brain," has greater deduction and reasoning power than the world's largest computer. It has been said by engineers, that if the brain's powers were duplicated, the computer would have to be as large as the Empire State Building.

Your brain is composed of thirty billion nerve cells (neurons). Each neuron links up with others in patterns to perform unlimited tasks. The psychobiological connection of brain and body is like an electromagnetic machine with the nervous system acting as transmitters.

Every cell of every organ, muscle, and nerve is influenced by the busy brain. The brain, in turn, reacts like a computer, influenced by what it is fed. Hypnosis is the skilled operator.

HYPNOSIS - THE BRAIN TRAINER

This wondrous computer-like brain is constantly exercising control over both the involuntary and voluntary systems of your body. It determines all of its action based on records and memories of past suggestion. With neuroscience permitting us incredible insight into brain function, we can now use hypnosis to manifest biological and psychological miracles which our forefathers would have considered pure magic.

While intelligence itself is instinctive, the art of using it must be learned. When we master hypnotic techniques, prospects are unlimited for increasing individual intelligence, as well as maximizing physical health. William James said it well: "Compared with what we ought to be, we are only half awake. Our fires are damped, our drafts are checked. We make use of only a small part of our mental and physical resources."

Hypnosis is the catalyst that can break the cords that tie us down to mediocrity. It can put us in touch with a section of the brain which enables us to become greater than our previous expectations of self. It takes one out of emotional confusion to rationality. More than a belief or philosophy, it is the gateway to highest consciousness, because each of us has, built into our brains, the machinery to enhance whatever we imagine and believe.

MASTER-MIND YOUR CORPUS CALLOSUM

Changes originate in subliminal visions. Thoughts and images are transmitted from images seen in the right brain to the left brain, via a band of nerve fibers called, "The Corpus Callosum." Within this cord, transmitters transport right brain messages to be put into action by the left brain. From there, directives are sent to the spinal cord and on through countless branches of nerves and blood vessels, until the messages reach a selected destination in the body.

The brain can be likened to a symphony orchestra. Each part plays under the leadership of its skillful conductor, the subconscious mind. Based on your thoughts, nerve connectors send out biochemicals with specific tasks that can make you happy, calm, energetic or, when negative, agitated or depressed. These busy transmitters put you to sleep at night and awaken you in the morning. They direct every thought, feeling and physical movement, as well as regulate the function of your organs. The confluence of energy is carried to every cell down to the tiniest atom. Hypnosis can help you to direct this power.

DEFINING THE TERM "HYPNOSIS"

Hypnosis has become an umbrella tern to cover a host of mental phenomena. First let's determine what hypnosis is not. It is not sleep; nor is it being awake; neither is it a coma, or supernatural. On the contrary, hypnosis is as natural as being asleep or being awake. Actually, it is a combination of the best of both. While the body seems to be at rest, the mind is keenly aware in the most intelligent way, and can direct messages to the body mechanisms. However, hypnosis can only take place when there is emotional readiness.

Internalizing with hypnosis can be accomplished on one's own or through the help of a therapist. It brings positive results whether in group or in a private session. Either way, it is effective in preparing the mind to accept constructive suggestion. The trance-state brings with it possibility thinking, which can give even the sickest and most depressed person hope that things will improve.

Without self-determination and inner control, our minds remain malleable to outside manipulation. On the other hand, Hypnotic techniques can help ordinary people accomplish extraordinary things. It can enable the disabled, uncover everyone's abilities and discover their hidden strength.

THE FOUR LEVELS OF HYPNOSIS

ONE... HYPNOIDAL (ALPHA) - This is a light level, easily attained by most people who have used meditation and guided imagery. It begins with muscle relaxation and brings with it a sense of contentment, as the heart rate slows down and harmonizes with the rhythm of deeper breathing. Concentration is enhanced, as well as memory recall.

TWO... STRESS REDUCTION (DEEP ALPHA) - There may be spontaneous eye closure, with inability to open the eyes at command. There is decreased motor activity of the limbs. There is drowsiness and lassitude; the operator lifts the subject's arm, which falls limply without resistance.

THREE... MENTAL/EMOTIONAL (LIGHT THETA) - As the trance deepens, the raised arm responds to suggestions of rigid catalepsy, and can remain in an upright position for a protracted length of time. Post hypnotic suggestion is accepted.

FOUR... CORE.. (DEEP THETA) - This is the Center Of Radiant Energy, an ultra- depth trance where our spirit manifests itself. Here, our minds reveal what our hearts may conceal. We awaken to the beauty of life and thrill to spiritual love. Referred in metaphysical literature as entering "The Third Eye," because the CORE provides enlightenment. Some call it, "an out-of-body-experience," or "Astral Projection."

Not everyone goes deeper than the Alpha level, especially the first time. This doesn't mean they can't be helped. Some people start off at a very light trance level and subsequently go a little deeper each time they practice. While theorists have divided depth into arbitrary groups, the fact is, most people's level fluctuates, somewhere in between categories.

Deep hypnosis has been considered by some old-time hypnotists as coma-like, (where the subject has no will, and is out of touch with conscious awareness). On the contrary, we now know the deepest level brings heightened consciousness. Twenty two years of direct experience has brought me to the realization that when it comes to correcting harmful human behavior, depth is secondary to the subject's motivation and the acceptance of responsibility to change for the better.

INWARD JOURNEY TO TRANSFORMATION

Hypnosis takes you on a fascinating trip into your mind and feelings, to discover how forces from the outside have programmed you. This is the space of reflection, as well as correction. Here you can de-condition and re-condition your reflexes. Decondition means you cleanse your mind of negative reflexes so that new positive conditioning can be instilled. When we learn to use hypnosis, we become inner-directed and self-protected against future negative suggestion.

Hypnosis is effective because it works with the natural function of the brain, spurred by the imagination. It takes us into a great warehouse of past accumulated information. Hypnotic introspection gives us control over our minds and the ability to accept or reject surrounding conditions. It brings insight to past experiences, present situations and future direction. Because it takes you right into the problem, and illuminates the cause, dramatic improvement happens in a fraction of the time it takes if you used traditional psychoanalysis.

YOU ARE MASTER OF YOUR MIND

What was not known to early mankind, and is of crucial importance is this: It is always the subject who allows the altered state of mind to happen, enabling the physical and emotional healing. The practitioner is merely a facilitator, who has been trained in techniques and methodology.

Can a person be forced into hypnosis? No. A person will not accept suggestion unless he has agreed to its application. Can anyone accomplish the amazing hypnotic state of heightened awareness? An emphatic, "Yes!" Hypnotic power is unique in each of us and universal to all. The state of hypnosis assures the highest form of receptivity of useful suggestion. It is the place where incoming information is evaluated, a cognitive way of by-passing obsolete blocks stuck in one's psyche.

In its ordinary state, the mind is occupied with sorting out the intrusions of outside impressions. Because of an overload of sensory input, (sight, sound, taste, smell, touch, our thought patterns can become scattered. Therefore, even the best of advice, received while in a sensory alert, conscious state, may go in one ear and out the other, without retention.

Thoughts are the tireless messengers racing from brain to body, via the spinal canal. The nerves send messages back to the brain. The brain then interprets, analyses, and makes its decision whether to accept or reject. A troublesome thought may be a fleeting one — even one word can be damaging.

SUGGESTION — ERASE AND REPLACE

You must choose whether you wish to perpetuate outmoded, unsatisfactory attitudes and responses or whether you are ready to embrace life fully. If the latter is true, there is nothing to stand in your way but yourself. Every time you think and every time you speak, you should know that each thought and word brings with it a reaction and a possible effect upon your body.

Suggestion has unlimited power in both directions. If your thoughts are of a defeatist nature, you are surely going to be defeated. However, if you think and speak as a winner, you cannot help but act like a winner and overcome obstacles.

Hypnosis works because we are each endowed with a unique gift — the ability to change our minds by using imagination. In a receptive state critical judgment is set aside and the belief system becomes an ally in the process. When this happens, hypnotic suggestion is eagerly carried out with the individual's intellectual and rational participation. Without self-empowerment, our minds are open to the negativity of others.

Not everyone goes into deep hypnosis, especially the first time. This doesn't mean they can't be helped. Some people start off at a very light trance level and subsequently go a little deeper, each time they practice. It was generally believed among practitioners that: "The deeper you go, the stronger the results." Twenty-two years of direct experience has brought me to the realization that depth of hypnotic trance is not always a criteria for best results.

Depth is secondary to the subject's motivation for change and willingness to accept suggestion. Some people who drift off into deep sleep during an induction are subconsciously avoiding responsibility that comes with changing. Positive suggestion can work dramatically even when the person is in a light, "hypnoidal" level. Whereas some deep subjects deliberately withdraw into a shell of armor and present no appreciable change for the better.

Of great importance to the success of hypnotherapy is the reciprocal interplay of empathetic energy between subject and therapist. The successful hypnotist soon learns that rapport must be established with the subject, because trust helps to accelerate results. To achieve trust, time must be taken to hear the complaints of the person with problems, without violating the subject's boundaries of communication. Don't pry unless invited.

THE BRAIN TO BODY CONNCTION

A large percentage of ailments have their origin in accumulated mental and physical tension. It is common knowledge that such illnesses as ulcers, headaches, and a host of other maladies are directly affected by stress. These are referred to as "psychosomatic illnesses," and according to some doctors seventy-five percent of physical symptoms fall into this category. Keep in mind that if your thoughts can make you sick, they can also make you well.

CONCIEVE-BELIEVE-ACHIEVE

It has long been known that visualization, without faith, cannot bring about the achievement. Without a strong belief system, images only stir up wishful-thinking. When we have positive confidence in the outcome, we are motivated to go after wanted results. Strong belief activates the psycho-biological connection of brain to body like an electromagnetic machine with the nervous system acting as transmitters. These nerve connectors send out biochemicals that can make you happy, calm, energetic and healthier in every way.

Hypnosis works because we are each endowed with a unique gift - the ability to change our minds by using imagination. While in a receptive state critical judgment is set aside and the belief system becomes an ally in the process. When this happens, a post-hypnotic command is eagerly carried out with the individual's intellectual and rational participation.

It has been postulated that hypnosis is a condition of emotional readiness during which perceptual alterations can be induced. It can only prove useful, however, when the individual has reached a stage of awareness of his own responsibility and capability to change. A favorable mental-set is a necessary precursor to the induction, or there will be subliminal resistance. Without self-involvement and inner control, our minds remain open to the manipulation of others.

THE INDUCTION TECHINIQUE

The hypnotist/teacher begins the procedure by putting the client at ease. Once trust is established, the subject is told: "Remove your shoes, belt, tie, glasses, watch, or anything else that restricts you."

The subject can recline on an easy chair, bed, or the floor. Try using pillows. Some people like them tucked under their knees, thighs, under the neck - others, not at all. Check posture for best results. Arms should be resting loosely with hands on the abdomen to monitor breathing. The legs should be separated with knees softly flexed. Here is a sample of relaxation patter that works well to prepare the subject to enter trance level to receive suggestion:

"Think of yourself as a limp rag doll, and let yourself go all over, like a puppet dangling on a string. Think of the joints of your skeletal frame as loosely separated. Pause for a moment and observe your body mentally. Are you holding back in some area? We all have some degree of muscle tension. When you locate your worst area you will be on your way to total relaxation by focusing into it. Muscle tension restricts the body's sense of ease. Think heaviness into the large muscles; the back muscles, the buttocks, and the thighs.

"Deliberately set aside conscious thinking about everyday problems, of yesterday, or tomorrow. All that matters is this moment - the here and now. Notice how good it feels to remove burdens from your mind and stress from your muscles. Your body is now generally relaxed and you are ready to learn how to enjoy a pleasant relaxing experience by allowing yourself to drift into a soothing state of serenity. It's so easy to lower stress when you have a method.

"You begin by focusing your eyes up toward the ceiling. That's good. Now, still keeping your eyes open, breath slowly and deeply. Place your hand on your lower torso and feel the rhythm of your breathing, the inhalation and exhalation.

"Take five deep breaths as I count backward from five to zero. Keep your eyes focused on a spot on the wall, up toward the ceiling. When you hear me say zero, that is a signal for you to close your eyes and just listen. Your eyelids may feel heavy and want to close, but wait until zero.

"Five... Take a deep breath...hold and breath out.
Four... Take another breath...hold and exhale. etc...
(continue to zero).

"That's right. Your eyes are softly closed now. You're doing just fine. Next, we are going to relax every part of your body, starting at the top of your head and working down to the tips of your toes. As I mention a part of your body, think about that part of you and let go. Breath in and out while focusing on each area that I call attention to."

Progressive relaxation is now suggested, starting from the top of the head and going down to the tips of the toes. Only when the subject is physically relaxed and mentally focused, will hypnotic suggestions be deeply absorbed.

Words used have to be carefully chosen to avoid negative connotation. The sound of the practitioner's voice can be authoritative or softly permissive. A good hypnotist knows which kind of delivery best suits the client's needs. My own approach is usually permissive. Unless a client asks for a strong, forceful session, I opt for treating him/her on an equal level, as an adult who shares in the responsibility of the induction.

RHYTHMIC BREATHING

After progressive relaxation has been accomplished, call attention to the rhythm of respiration. Focusing into breathing is essential to any deep meditation. Not only is inhalation important, exhalation should be sufficiently strong so that it expels not only carbon dioxide and impurities, but accumulated muscle tension, as well. When the lungs are only partially emptied, they can only be partially refilled. Hypnotist:

"Now that you have relaxed the musculature of your body, focus on your breathing apparatus. Place your right hand on your lower abdomen, about mid-way between the end of your ribcage and the navel. Observe how you breathe in and breathe out. Check to make sure that you are not moving the upper chest muscles.

"Remember, only the abdomen moves, not the chest and not the shoulders. They are immobilized, detached from your thoughts. Focus into the area around your navel. Notice how the lower diaphragm muscles push out as you fill your body with oxygen. Now pull your abdomen in and force your lungs to expel the air slowly. You are now in touch with your reflexes through your respiratory system.

DEEPEN THE RHYTHM OF YOUR BREATHING

- Inhale slowly to the count of five.
- Hold the breath for one or two counts.
- Release the breath to the count of five.
- Rest for five counts and repeat over again.

Whereas, the count of five is an easy tempo to establish, it helps develop greater stamina and mind-control when one can extend the count in the following manner:

- Ten inhaling, five hold,
- Ten exhaling, ten hold.

This is Yoga-type breathing and is very beneficial. Once you have relaxed your body and are breathing deeply and rhythmically, your mind opens for positive thoughts. Having gone through the process of "unwinding" the knots, you are now open for self-realization. During regular practice periods, once your mind and body are tranquil and relaxed, repeat just one suggestion again and again. Fifty to one hundred repetitions in a day, is not too much. The more repetition, the better, and the sooner improvement will show itself.

HYPNOSIS IS INDUCED BY FOLLOWING THESE EIGHT STEPS:

1...**Eye Fixation -** The focus might be any object, or simply a spot on the ceiling. This eliminates the impute of images from the outside and increases mental concentration. Focusing the gaze is the first step toward internalizing one's thoughts.

2...**Monitored Breathing -** The subject is now in touch with the rhythmic action of the lungs. This expanded respiration exercise, becomes the foundation for the next step.

3...Progressive Body Relaxation - This procedure may start at the top of the head and go down to the toes, or vice versa. No matter which direction is employed, the effect is to release body stress.

4...Deepening Techniques - The more profound the trance level, the stronger the helpful suggestion takes hold. Deepening methods include visualizations, countdowns and use of the Alphabet. These will be detailed later in this book.

5...Applied Suggestion - Depending on the subject's needs, suggestion is repeated many times during the session. We must de-condition old pattern and then recondition the autonomic nervous system to behave automatically in a better way.

6...Visualization - Our physical, mental and emotional well being is formed by the images we see. During hypnosis, the wanted result are conjured up in the mind's eye, which spurs the mechanics of changeover from negative to positive.

7...Post-Hypnotic Suggestion - For the benefit to be long lasting, the subject is given a suggestion to reinforce his program. A trigger word or action is suggested. For example: "Each time you drink a glass of water, you will feel full and satisfied." Or - "Whenever you see a person smoking, you will tell yourself: That's not for me."

8...Coming Out of the Trance - The induction takes the subject from an awake level to a trance level. At the close of the session the process is reversed. A count from one to ten repeats the conditioning, so upon awakening, positive thoughts are uppermost in the subject's alert mind. There is a translucent clarity, a sense that a load has been removed from one's shoulders. There follows a day of joy, expanding beyond mundane tasks that must be performed. A subject said: "I felt my spirits soar."

The state of hypnosis assures the highest receptivity of useful suggestion. It is the place where incoming information-to-be-acted-upon is evaluated and combined with stored data from the environment. It is a cognitive way of bypassing blocks that stand in the way of higher achievements.

TECHNIQUES AND METHODOLOGY

In addition to the induction process which takes you into the trance-state, there are techniques that focus on problem solving from womb to tomb; from painless birth to extending everyone's life span. In fact, hypnosis is being used even before birth. Prenatal suggestion to the unborn will be one of the wonders of the new century.

Hypnosis has already proved effective in optimizing not only the infant's wellness, but energizing the mother both physically and mentally. I have never heard of a woman who use hypnosis as part of her birthing experience complain, of post-partum depression. The sooner the expectant mother learns how to talk to parts of her body, the easier the delivery and the emotional state that follows.

You can instruct a chosen part of your anatomy to behave as you tell it to. This is called differential relaxation and enables a person to focus attention on one part of the body while the rest remains detached and immobile. Acquiring the art of focused relaxation takes practice, but it is well worth the effort, for you will find that it improves your health in specific ways, like recovery from accidents, or physical dysfunction.

"Begin by closing your eyes, slowly and softly. As you close your eyes, consciously shut out any thoughts, images, or impressions from the outside. You are going to get together with a specific area that you wish to see instant health-normalcy — perfect function. Take three deep breaths, ever so slowly and very deeply. At the last exhalation, picture your mind-screen and see the result that you want. Hold the visualization as you count down from fifty to zero. If the image fades bring it back again."

MIRROR TECHNIQUE FOR SELF ESTEEM

Our physical, mental and emotional well being is formed by the images we see. Encouraging oneself by praise helps build confidence. Compliments and even self-flattery can help strengthen a weak ego. Sometimes it is necessary to do so to compensate for the downgrade we are often subjected to.

Your mind is unlimited in its ability to take your own thought and turn it into personalized progress. Sometimes you must take a thought and make it happen, otherwise a negative rut will ensnare. During hypnosis, the wanted result are conjured up in the mind's eye, which spurs the mechanics of changeover from negative to positive. While looking in a mirror, look into your eyes and speak your auto suggestions out loud. Positive suggestion spoken out loud is dramatically effective. Looking at yourself as you speak also involves the sense of sight, which makes the affirmation even stronger.

Imagery is the art of using fantasy to conjure up mind-pictures that can later serve as a guide in real-life situations. your imagination can also erase thoughts of possible failure and fear of inadequacy. You can replace negative fantasies with visions of success. That key is your warehouse of accumulated memories, some of which are useful, others useless. Other people's suggestions as well as your own are recorded there in detail throughout your lifetime.

How this information determines one's lifestyle depends on which memories one recalls. Harnessing the creative force of mind power and putting it to work is not difficult if you follow the methods, clearly described in this book.

CALENDAR TECHNIQUE TO REACH GOALS

Notice a calendar on the wall see the goal date that you have set for reaching your best weight and improved image. Now get on a scale and weigh yourself. See that you have reached your goal. See yourself as a clothes model modeling clothes in the size you prefer. The audience applauds.

If you are a student, see the date of graduation and how

well respected you are. You can also use the calendar to store social engagements and hw you wish them to please you. The calendar technique works in many situations.

SEE A MOVIE OR TELEVISION SCREEN

This is a also a great technique to help you look into your future to create the kind of life that you want, without troubles or obstacles. If you are handicapped by lack of funds or helpful connections, this method will bring you some surprising answers.

THE PERSONAL COMPUTER METHOD

Each of us has, built into our brains the machinery to disclose whatever information we need to know. The brain has many compartments, each with its own special function. You can log on to any of them with the computer visualization. Imagine a picture of your brain and connect to the area you need to master. You don't need to be a medical student for this to work. Fantasize your personal image of your brain.

Create your own software. Just ask the all-knowing, "Higher Intelligence." (See it listed as one of your favorites) Type in your questions and conduct a SEARCH. Watch the solution appear on the monitor of your mind.

FINGER TAPPING TECHNIQUE

While sitting and waiting anywhere, in someone's office, or at a red light while driving, any place at all, silently mouth the sugges tions over and over again as you tap your forefinger with each repetition. This physical gesture instills the idea of success even deeper into the autonomic nervous system.

"LAYING-ON-HANDS"- AS OLD AS TIME

Some techniques date back thousands of years to the early Egyptian healing temples. Here are a few that are still popular with modern hypnotists:

1. Making hand-passes over the body, has a placebo effect of deepening the trance. The healer does not touch, and informs the subject of the action.

2. Laying on hands is a type of touch therapy and helps the hypnotized subject focus on a troubled area that needs increased circulation.

3. Using objects like crystals, stones, talisman, etc. When people believe an object has healing powers, it can act as a spur to help them improve. Some hypnotists give the client a crystal to hold to add to a sense of serenity.

CHAPTER 3

"CORE" - CENTER OF RADIANT ENERGY

Change Your Mind and Change Your Life
Tap Family History - Solve Its Mystery

CORE is the deepest state of hypnosis. At this depth of meditation, a person can heal the physical body and mend the injured mind. This is the place where the genius of invention and creative artistry are born. It awakens that divine spark of genius that differentiates humans from other creatures and gives meaning to everything we accomplish. CORE boosts intuition, provides insight to the past, wisdom for the future, and solutions to every-day problems.

The dictionary defines CORE in many interesting ways. In the area of geology, it is referred to as the center of the earth. The earth's CORE is a mass of magnetic fluid composed of iron and nickel, which ensures life on the planet, due to its force of gravity. Without it, we would merely be atoms floating aimlessly in outer space. Regarding vegetation, CORE is appropriately described as: "The center where seeds are stored, in order to extend new life." It works that way for people, too.

The hypnotic CORE provides pinpoint focus. It can be likened to the eye of a storm; there is safety and calm in the center, even though the winds are raging around it. Hypnotic CORE is not only a safe-place, but also a quiet place where a spiritual connection takes place. In this state of bliss, the body is inert as if asleep, while at the same time the energy of the brain is optimized to function creatively.

One's CORE is the place to explore solutions to problems and gain the power to make the best choices for an expanded life. Within this cradle of higher consciousness, intelligence monitors every thought and movement. Safe in this womb of wellness, you become inner directed and self-protected against negative input.

In CORE, the outer layers of perceptions, conceptions, pretensions and environmental programming are assessed with higher intelligence. Everything that you have warehoused, based on other peoples' expectations are examined under a new light. In a state of NOW, time is suspended and anxieties cease to exist. Reaching your center opens the mind to dramatically change habits, by altering reactions in the nervous system. At this depth, the brain releases endorphins. Studies indicate that endorphins have a chemical structure similar to morphine and it is here that pain is lessened and healing becomes intensified.

DEEPENING FROM MEDIUM TO CORE

Once a person has experienced a medium trance, they are ready to enter a new dimension, which is the deepest state of self-controlled trance. This can be accomplished on one's own, or with the help of a professional hypnotist. The simplest method of deepening is the "countdown technique." There are many variations of this technique. Here are a few:

1... **Descending a Staircase** - "Visualize yourself at the top of a winding staircase. There are twenty steps. You hold the banister and count off the steps as you go down deeper... twenty... take a deep breath...exhale and take another step down and go deeper...nineteen..." (continue repetition).

2... **Elevator Technique** - "You are facing the doors of an elevator on the tenth floor. You step into the elevator and the doors close. You see a wall-panel with the floor numbers clearly marked. Push the button nine, and go down to the ninth floor. There, the doors open and you see a sign - GO

DEEPER TO REACH CORE. The doors close, you push eight and go down deeper...Continue until you reach one, the doors open and you see a sign - YOU ARE IN YOUR CORE."

3... **Down Into a Peaceful Valley** - "You are standing at the top of a hill looking down into a beautiful valley. You descend down the gradual slope of the green hillside into the valley. As you take each step you count down from twenty to zero. You stroll among the trees until you find a hammock between two trees. Relax into the hammock as you feel a breeze sway the branches of the trees, you go deeper into CORE.

4... **The Alphabet Technique** - Here we substitute numbers for the letters of the alphabet. "Imagine that you are standing in front of a blackboard, a chalk in one hand, an erasure in the other. Each time you write and erase a letter you go deeper. You write the letter A...and you erase the letter A...and go deeper... You write the letter B...and you erase the letter B... (and so forth till the letter Z). The words appear: "Enter CORE."

CORE HYPNOSIS IS HEALING

While the normally healthy body has fantastic recuperative power, some people test it to the extreme degree. The body goes through a process of revitalization while you are in your deepest meditation. It is then that the renewal of tissue takes place, as the free radical cells of illness are diminished. There has been a great deal of discussion in the media, pointing to the fact that an overwhelming percentage of physical ailments have their origin in negative mental attitudes.

The multitude of ways the mind's emotions affect the body is legendary. Nowhere is this more evident than in the phenomenon of religious passion which brings about stigmatic scarring.

CORE AND RELIGIOUS STIGMATA

Few people, religious or otherwise, are aware of the connection between the mind-set during prayer and the hypnotic trance. Research has established that visualization, when combined with passionate emotion, brings about physical changes. A simple example might be speaking to a shy person in a suggestive manner and they manifest their feeling by blushing.

Stigmata is a fascinating example of the extreme power of suggestion in bringing about physical changes based on visual imagery. Religious writers describe stigmata as a reproduction of the wounds that Christ received on the cross. Stigmata were once believed to be replicas of the wounds and/or scars, which were supernaturally induced. This premise has lead Catholic Popes to bestow the honor of Sainthood upon the stigmatized.

Not all cases have been authenticated as miracles, however. A distinction is made by the church, between scars caused by mental imagery alone, and those spiritually imposed. Theologians do not ignore the possibility that the power of the mind may be involved in bodily changes. Those of us who work holistically to help cure psychosomatic illness, know from experience, the brain's connection to physical changes.

We know that whenever a suggestion is repeated over and over again, it becomes a conditioned reflex and takes root in the autonomic nervous system. It is the nervous system that carries the messages to specific parts of the body. This is why people who learn to enter CORE can correct serious maladies.

HYPNOSIS IS GOING MAINSTREAM

Hypnosis is no longer considered controversial, propounded only by a narrow segment of Nu-Age healers. Traditional medical doctors are also using its benefits to accelerate healing. They are also at the forefront in the newest research, and it's going on all over the world. Here's some interesting, information based on a report printed in the *Prevention Magazine:*

A number of deep hypnosis studies performed at the University of Manchester, England and then the Eastern Virginia Medical School in Norfolk, proved CORE hypnosis can bring great improvement in the internal organs. Patients suffering from intestinal disorders reported less pain, less bloating, better elimination, freedom from anxiety and general well being.

An identical deep induction script was used, with the same healing suggestions given to each of the eighteen subjects. After the hypnotist produced the deep level, he suggested pinpoint focus, which he refers to as: "Gut-directed imagery." There were seven sessions given, each lasting for forty minutes. Of the eighteen subjects used in the test, seventeen reported excellent results.

CORE depth, which most people attain with regular practice, can eliminate many preventable deaths. Here is a report published in the *Journal of the American Medical Association:*

ESTIMATED NUMBER OF DEATHS CAUSED PER YEAR
BY PREVENTABLE LIFESTYLE BEHAVIOR:

TOBACCO	400,000
DIET-WEIGHT	300,000
ALCOHOL	100,000
FIREARMS	35,000
SEX DISEASES	30,000
MOTOR VEHICLES	25,000
ILLICIT DRUGS	20,000

While hypnosis opens up a vast array of possibilities for cure, it is in the drug addiction area that responds rapidly beyond all other alternative correctional methods. Millions of people are now addicted. *Time magazine* published this list of users in 1997 and the count is rising:

HEROIN USERS	200,000
AMPHETAMINES	800,000
COCAINE/CRACK	1.5 million
MARIJUANA	10 million
ALCOHOL	11 million (abusers)
NICOTINE	61 million

All of these chemicals have side effects that can lead to ill health and premature death. The human body and it's excellent brain, receive no benefit and lose natural function. Billions of dollars are being wasted trying to cure preventable disease resulting from self-inflicted addicted behavior. It would be to the advantage of our economy if we offered hypnosis classes to avoid this waste of money and human life. Disease prevention with the human mind would costs less than five percent of the cost of cure in medical facilities.

CENTERING BRINGS BALANCE AND HARMONY

CORE hypnosis is a natural method to stay healthy and reach a place of inner peace and tranquillity. It releases power inherent in all of us. This is where we learn truth based on objective reality, while examining the hard facts. CORE not only revitalizes mind and body, it assures your birthright to be the best that you can be — ever growing, everlasting unlimited happiness, fulfillment of goals, to assure yourself a life of love and prosperity. You will nurture talents you didn't even know you had.

CORE will enable you to use specialized methods to travel back in time, not to only early childhood, but even past life. No matter how far back you are able to regress, it will be beneficial because it brings understanding of events based on the cause and effect upon you.

When we learn to reach and strengthen the CORE or our higher mind, we become focused, re-energized, bolstered against negative suggestion and destructive conditioning which threatens each of us in an individual way.

Hypnosis takes us to the source of power and gives us control over our surrounding conditions. It is the greatest adventure to one's unknown strength which lies dormant within each of us. Socrates advise: "Know thyself," becomes a reality when you experience your depth. Without knowing ourselves and what makes our mental machinery tick, we can neither solve our problems, nor adapt and live in harmony with the world around us. When negative feelings have no outlet, tension is transferred to the muscle tissue, nerves and inner organ of the body.

Anxious anticipation of possible failure, suspicion of other people's motives, and other negative feelings like guilt, shame, and worry, all cause a physical reaction. Tests show that muscles tighten their grip on the nerves and blood vessels that flow to vital organs, like the heart. A pattern of pressure results, until a sort of armor is built up in areas of the body.

Restoration of health demands the loosening of this stranglehold; the freeing of the constricting bind of muscle, to nerves and organs. With proper circulation, nerve sensibility, and mobility can be restored. CORE is remarkable for expediting the therapeutic process of breaking through barriers. Its powers are phenomenal, enriching our lives and stretching boundaries, as we discover the significance of our behavior upon our health and how to change that behavior, to enrich life.

TIME TO OPEN AND EXPAND YOUR MIND

In its ordinary state, the mind is occupied with mostly sorting out the intrusions of unimportant outside impressions. Thought patterns become scattered. Therefore, even the best of advice received while in a conscious state, may go in one ear and out the other, non-directed, without a destination.

Any person who consistently practices hypnosis, will eventually reach his/her deepest level of receptivity to changing. In CORE, the outer layers of perceptions, conceptions, pretensions and environmental conditioning are easily assessed with higher intelligence. Only when you reveal what is buried within, can you release your mind-power from its accumulated residual debris. This profound level of hypnosis takes us into a great warehouse of accumulated information, gives us control over our minds and the ability to accept or reject surrounding conditions. It brings intuitive insight to past experiences, present situations and future direction. Because it takes you right into the center of problems, it illuminates and eliminates the causes. Dramatic positive changes take place quickly.

It is a cognitive way of by-passing blocks stuck in your psyche; a state of NOW, where time is suspended and anxieties cease to exist. Within CORE, you are inner directed and self-protected against negative input. Reaching your CORE allows you to sponge out trauma, toxins and tension and to make a fresh start in life. Within this space, transmitters transport right brain messages put into action by the left brain.

From there, directives are sent to the brain-stem which merges into the spinal cord and on through countless branches of nerves, until the messages reach a selected destination in the body. In this way, the inner you enhances the outer you, by bringing insight as to the cause of dysfunction. Reaching the trance level opens the subliminal mind to reconstructive programming though retraining the triggers that set off reactions in the nervous system, which in turn regulates behavior.

CORE hypnosis is a self-induced condition where positive images act as maps that lead to higher consciousness. In order to understand how it can help you (and everyone you know), to rapidly change for the better, experiment with the various levels of hypnotic induction, until you reach your deepest space. You will know when you get there. In a meditative state of CORE, you can hear and recognize what the real truth is for you. You come face-to-face with your own unique, personal truth based on objective reality and hard facts. The realness of truth about yourself, your unlimited potential, your true responsibilities to yourself and others.

EXPLORE THE POWER IN YOUR CENTER

If you picture the sun radiating energy in all directions, you can better imagine the integrated power that we each possess. This magnetic energy can be extended outward as "centripetal" force or reversed as "centrifugal", which means drawing in to one's center whatever we need from the external environment. Centering brings balance and harmony. It is the area with equal distance in all directions. A pivot point, where there is calm at the axis; around which everything else rotates, revolves and radiates. You are the sun of your own solar system. It is a most dependable part of you, always available; a place of calm and introspection, inspiration and motivation.

Here are some reactions from people who have reached CORE hypnosis and given up substance addiction:

"I felt naturally high, inside a space of detached spiritual serenity. The calmness stays afterwards and makes you aware of your power to ignore stuff you don't need."

"Core helps to direct your mental energy force into action. I used it to visualize my body the way I wanted it to look, firm and younger. My vision became my reality."

"I used it for peace of mind and improved my sleep. Also for the first time in my life I am sticking to a health diet and exercise regularly, which has always been a problem with me."

"Hypnosis gave me the confidence to give up alcohol and other drugs by directing my mind away from self-indulgence. It also opened up my natural resources."

"For me, psyching myself has protected me from external tension from other people which in the past pushed me into eating binges. Now I know how to bypass the stress without sweets or other useless harmful foods."

"I felt as if I was in a dream state directing my mind to visualize how much better I could look and feel."

You can give suggestions to yourself either verbally (out loud) or non-verbally (silently). Both methods are effective in breaking down the wall of negative resistance. Advocates of auto-suggestion say suggestion spoken out loud is most powerful. To implant the suggestion even deeper, tap your forefinger with each repetitive suggestion. This technique brings together the mid and body, while at the same time tapping the thought into the automatic motor system.

Silent suggestion can be practiced effectively no matter where we happen to be, without anyone even being aware that we are doing it. Each time you make a self-improvement suggestion to your mind, you accumulate the power of this activating force and teach your mind to flash the right messages to you in time of need. We owe it to ourselves as thinking human beings, to use our reason to elevate not only personal satisfaction but also express broader humanistic caring.

CORE DRAMATICALLY REDUCES STRESS

Deep hypnosis, performed with regularity, can wipe the slate clean of a lifetime of residual physical and emotional trauma. Unresolved tension is a harsh master over the human body. It ties the nerves into knots and they accumulate into a barricade that shuts off sensibility and blood circulation. It also causes the body to lose its natural rhythmic pulsations.

Lowering stress is like releasing a compressed spring, strong feeling bounces upward and away from past crippling restrictions. Once you have freed them, your senses will continually make your life a creative experience. Sensory awareness can restore the missing links of lost identity. Subliminal sensory perception brings with it the soul's awakening, and can make a disjointed person whole again.

Past patterns of thinking always haunt the present, if you let them. While most people know that a person is molded by early precepts, they are less aware people can and do change. All that is required is a strong desire to have it happen. Change can only begin by changing one's attitude.

Attitude + Action = Achievement.

OVER-INDULGENCE SHORTENS LIFE

Moderation in all things is life-extending, but few Americans live as minimalists. Eighty percent eat copious amounts of non-nourishing foods. Our culture makes us prey to mercenary interests that conduct massive advertising campaigns to condition us into - Over eating... Over smoking... Over drinking... Over straining and - Under living. What is so deplorable is that the average person is not even aware of this unconscious control. The problem with food obsession, alcohol and drugs, is that many people who use them do not think of them as a problem, and they are right! It's not a problem if they practice hypnosis and discover the power of centering into their CORE.

KICKS HAVE SERIOUS KICKBACKS

Our bodies are not equipped to handle smoke. From the most elementary point of view, it is certainly not natural for a person to breathe into his lungs the pollution from burning weeds of any kind, whether it be commercial cigarettes, a homemade joint, or whatever. Nature didn't intend it that way. Any of the other animal species (who are supposedly of a lower mental capacity) run from smoke because they sense it is deadly.

The lungs have an important job to do. They must supply sufficient oxygen to the brain and body for healthy cell renewal and rejuvenation. For example, it is simple common sense to realize that people who smoke marijuana are harming themselves, just as they would smoking tobacco. The argument that smoking pot is healthier than smoking regular cigarettes doesn't hold water in view of the latest reports from researchers.

The following factors link marijuana to other drugs:

1... It is illegal, part of the drug culture, punishable by law.

2... As a relaxant, it lowers resistance to the harder stuff.

3... It is psychologically addictive and acts as a crutch.

There is a great deal of research now going on to determine just what long-range effects the use of pot has on the nervous system and the body's vital organs. The U.S. government is involved in dozens of study programs in major cities throughout the country. In addition, there are over two hundred other investigations going on privately, both here and abroad. Among the early findings are indications that marijuana, in continued use, may cause injury to the brain. It would take years, even generations, to truly test all the ramifications involved.

GIVE YOURSELF A GOOD TALKING TO

What we say and the sound that has the greatest affect upon us at all times is the sound of our own voice. Because it is the closest sound to our mental receptors, it influences our behavior greatly. Notice how your own positive affirmations affects you.

Suggestion is not merely words that are spoken, your own behavior also acts as a conditioning factor. The conversion from physical distress to feeling "better than ever" will work for most people. However, there are some who will become seriously ill even though they know that there is no basis for their suffering. This points up the validity of the psychosomatic theory that all illness begins in the mind.

Hypnosis puts us in touch with a section of the brain which is higher than the conscious self. It brings us the power to become greater than our expectations of self. The confluence of energy is carried to every cell down to the tiniest atom. There's a universal, worldwide need for the kind of higher consciousness that CORE hypnosis provides.

CORE HELPS YOU BOOST YOURSELF!

Self-realization seldom happens spontaneously. We have been drilled to be ashamed of self-praise, yet it's only appreciation that can raise and re-mold the limited way in which we think about ourselves. Encouraging oneself by praise helps restore confidence. Compliments and even self-flattery can help strengthen a weak ego. Sometimes it is necessary to do so to compensate for the downgrading we may have been subjected to.

Where do negative thoughts come from? Like a tree, just as much substance is invisible as is showing above the surface. Our branches are only the projection of the kind of roots that they have sprung from. Where has your self-image, your identity come from? What sort of soil was it nurtured by?

Thoughts take root and grow in the pattern determined by environment. A tree's branches, twigs, even the tiniest leaves are like ideas. They are the thoughts and words expressing the manner in which the seeds were sowed. Buds blossom and flowers turn to fruit and whether that fruit is sweet or bitter depends on the nutrients fed to it.

Inertia comes with blaming others. This is the way all habit is formed, whether it be cigarettes, alcohol, or sexual dysfunction. Failure is also a habit; all habit is self-made, and can be self-broken. The procedure is the same.

... First: The mind accepts an idea, then...

... Second: The body puts it into action, and...

... Third: The repeated action becomes a habit.

Breaking an unwanted habit means reeducating your body's reflexes. You are the only one that can bring this change about because motivation is the foundation of change. The changeover from negative expectations to positive ones is accomplished through carefully worded, concise thoughts, which are repeated just before entering the hypnotic level, and reinforced throughout the session.

Auto-suggestion can be stated at intervals all through the day, in a waking state. It is the best way to affirm your determination and assert that you are moving toward practical goals. Before you begin to formulate suggestions to yourself, ask yourself:

What have I been telling myself about myself?

Where did my ideas about myself come from?

Why do I lack confidence? When did it start?

The right suggestions make things happen in the right way, to suit your individuality. Cicero said, "Nobody can give you wiser advice than you, yourself." There is no voice more powerful than your own when it is motivated for self-fulfillment. The most helpful thing to tell yourself is "Yes, I Can!"

Here are some general suggestions that you can repeat during your periods of self-talk, as well as prior to induction into hypnosis. The more often you focus on these good thoughts, the sooner you will see dramatic improvement. Eventually you may be able to give yourself commands at will, as many practitioners do. Once your mind has been fed these image builders, the feedback will help you overcome fear of failure. Keep in mind that the most dominant thought focused upon is the one that is apt to come about. Just before closing your eyes and relaxing your body, repeat any or all of the following basic self-suggestions:

... I have everything that it takes to fulfill my life.

... I have no trouble getting cooperation when I need it.

... I will reach my maximum capacity of success in all ways.

Repetition turns autosuggestion into reality. The more often you give yourself self-building suggestions, the sooner results will manifest themselves. This process does not take extra time. Simply incorporate suggestive conditioning into your daily routine. Positive thinking should be going on all the time, any time and anywhere.

During your regular practice periods, once your mind and body are tranquil and relaxed, repeat just one suggestion again and again. Fifty to one hundred repetitions is not too much. The more the better, and the sooner improvement will show itself.

REHEARSAL TECHNIQUE

Self-Imagery is the art of using fantasy to conjure up mind-pictures that can later serve as a guide in real-life situations. An improved image builds confident expectations that can turn the tide from merely wanting to succeed to actually doing so. A good reminder is... First you view it — then you do it!

The mind's perception of improvement speeds the relearning process, even though the perception is only in the imagination. Your imagination can also erase thoughts of impending failure and fear of inadequacy. You can replace negative fantasies with visions of success. Harnessing the creative force of mind power and putting it to work for happiness is not difficult if you follow the method clearly described in this book.

DISCOVER TRUTH IN DREAMS

Visionary meditation has been practiced by mankind, through the ages, since the beginning of history. The basic difference between these ancient pastimes and the methods described in this book is the difference between strictly spiritual meditation and meditation to bring the body and mind into harmony with spirit.

We are concerned here with the latter, at this time, for unless the body is in healthy function the spirit cannot be well, either. Instead of escaping from responsibility by mental detachment, we are going to take you in the other direction, the confrontation of your life force. Creative CORE meditation can and will do the job of retraining your mind and body to work with universal energy.

Deliberately meditating on reveries and recollections from the past can reveal profound answers to troublesome questions. Deep hypnosis gives you the power to select a topic important to you and to deliberately dream images around that topic. You will be able to ask of your subconscious mind, "What is the significance of this reverie?"

The Talmud says, "A dream not understood is like an unopened letter to yourself." If you wish, you can grow out of inhibiting mind barriers into a radiant world of limitless vistas by opening some of the "unopened letters to yourself."

To establish harmonious concert between body and mind, you must first withdraw bad images from the corners of your memory bank. Then discard them as useless debris and deposit better ones in their stead. You can draw excellent dividends from this mind bank and enrich every phase of living.

CHAPTER 4

SUBLIMINAL PERSUASION BY MEDIA

Television Images Invade The Mind
Addictive Habits Can Be Eliminated

Television is both pervasive and persuasive. Millions of Americans have their television switched on most of the day. Some leave it on, from the moment they awaken until they fall asleep. The American Institute of Mental Health reports: "Over one-third of adults watch more than four hours of television each day." Another study reveals that more than two million children under eleven are still watching at midnight.

Television has become the baby-sitter for working mothers. By the time a child reaches his/her teens, that child has been influenced by 10 to 15 thousand hours of suggestion. Much of what they see is people with unhealthy habits and violent behavior. The TV screen is a place where the oddities and illnesses of the world are visually emphasized. After a while, inappropriate behavior seems normal and acceptable to children, as well as in their adulthood.

Surveys say that 99% of American households have at least one television set;

some have as many as five. Television images are the most powerful influence in our lives today, and can help us or harm us. Unfortunately, the later is more often true. Vulgarity after vulgarity coarsens the viewer's mind. Contents of shows are ratings driven and pander to the wishes of manufacturers who market their products for profit.

Television, in just a few decades, has become the dominant influence in most of our lives. It is the teacher of the young, molder of teenage violent behavior and perpetrator of family dysfunction. It not only enters the home, it enters the viewer's subconscious mind. Concerned parents struggle with this invading force as they try to raise their children to be less violent and avoid addictions. Studies show television has become more of a role model than parents, because the time parents spend with kids is less than the time kids spend in front of the tube.

SUBLIMINAL INVADER-PERSUADERS

It's a gruesome thought, but the media, depends on mass addiction to perpetuate it economy. Its basic role is to create consumers; its very existence demands this interaction. When a viewer says, "I think," is the person actually doing the thinking or repeating someone else's thinking? Most of the time people think what they have been taught to think. What they say today is often what they've heard yesterday. People grow up parroting someone else's opinions; they walk the streets like robots, unaware they are victims of mind-control.

Repetitive advertising becomes mesmerizing. It's sugar coated with amusement, but not so funny when viewers get hooked on sweets, caffeine, tobacco, alcohol and other bad products. Analysts describe this process as adaptation and mental accommodation. Pill popping, alcohol and smoking seem normal to young people because they've watched 'nice' people do it on television again and again.

The commercials assume we are all sick, and need some sort of medical product to recover. Rarely do they tell you how to avoid illness. What is so deplorable is that the average person is not even aware of this subliminal intrusion into the crevices of the mind. When young people become acclimated to hearing the virtues of over-the counter-drugs, they tend to be open to street drugs, as well.

STREET DRUGS ARE READILY AVAILABLE

Narcotics range from stimulants to depressants, to hallucinogens. There are variations of cannabis, inhalants, cocaine and crack. Combined with alcohol, the user can lose control of his/her mind. The final consequences can destroy his/her entire family, (as well as one's liver and other internal organs). There are over 60 dangerous drugs easily available and in wide use, as we have pointed out in the previous chapter. Dependency is a symptom of deeper disturbances, which the troubled person needs to correct. That's why everyone needs to know about the help they can get from hypnosis.

Unless we filter out what should be rejected; unless we make a habit of sorting out the negative from the positive, we will always be mastered by others. If we don't deliberately reject outside suggestion, it affects us as if it were our own. Other people's thoughts become internalized and ingrained, especially if repeated often enough. This is the way all habit is formed, whether it be cigarettes, alcohol, or any dependency. The enemy from the outside nurtures the enemy that resides within.

FAMILY ACCEPTANCE OF ACOHOL AND DRUGS

We are witnessing a socialization of addiction and self-destructive behavior. Often, persons who come from a family with addictions, find themselves repeating the same patterns. These patterns seem comfortable and acceptable because they were learned from family role models. Most people never realize they are being programmed.

They have lost control because anything accepted by our subconscious, becomes internalized. Once a suggestion is accepted and carried out, it begins urging to be repeated and reinforced. Eventually, what was once outside suggestion is internalized.

Fortunately, what was once learned is not necessarily permanent. The mind is like a tape recorder — you can erase and replace the space with better programming.

You can unchain your brain and retrain it.

The effort to get beneath the threshold of rational thinking, has even spread to commercial messages that spin by so fast that they flash into the mind past our conscious guard. Alterations of thought patterns lead to changes in behavior which has resulted in shocking self-destructive habits. Victims who lack awareness, are constantly influenced not only by outside stimuli such as television, newspapers, but also other people's opinions. Knowingly or unknowingly, we are continually bombarded by negative suggestion which pollutes our minds.

Much of negative suggestion harms us without our even knowing it is taking place. Party drinking is by far the most common image on the screen. Of the eighty-five percent of Americans who drink, most of them imbibe for social reasons. Out of that group, twenty to thirty million are hooked on spirits for "stimulation." It doesn't really help, either to stimulate or to relax. Actuarial tables show that alcoholics have twelve fewer years of life, and those years can hardly be called living. Alcoholism, more than any other symbol of man's inhumanity toward himself, is proof of the power of negative suggestion.

We have all been coaxed, cajoled, and conditioned into thinking of drinking as a fun, partying thing to do. Billions of advertising dollars have been spent convincing us of this lie. Unlike street drugs and marijuana, alcohol has social acceptance. People who promote its use should visit a hospital and observe the babies born suffering from the Fetal Alcohol Syndrome. Born addicted, their tiny, undersized bodies quiver, as their damaged brains struggle to survive.

THE POWER OF UNAWARE SUGGESTION

Here is an interesting example of mass suggestibility which occurred at a San Diego military base. The headline in a local newspaper read:

"1,000 SOLDIERS GET SICK FROM RUMOR THAT WASN'T TRUE".

The case reported in the *American Journal of Epidemiology*, explains that the recruits at the base heard and read a false rumor that they had been exposed to an airborne toxic poison. Mass hysteria resulted and caused hundreds to have the same symptoms. (The case was unusual because most cases of mass hysteria that have been reported, have been about women.)

As the rumor spread, more and more young men started coughing and complaining of chest pains which set off a domino effect on hundred of soldiers. Finally, authorities were forced to evacuate 1,800 of the men who had trouble breathing. Over 350 soldiers of those were taken by ambulance to a hospital for testing. Eight men felt so ill, they were actually hospitalized for several days. When clinical tests were done, the results showed there was nothing wrong with the air or the men.

In cases like this, strong counter-suggestion is given under hypnosis to wipe out the negative imprint. The conversion from physical distress to feeling "better than ever" will work for most people. However, there are some who become seriously ill even though, they know there is no basis for their suffering. This points up the validity of the psychosomatic theory that illness begins in the mind.

Repetitive suggestion works even when the viewer is in a light, hypnoidal level, which is what happens when we watch television. The mind opens up to record images while we focus into the lighted screen. Suggestion is not merely words spoken, watching other people's behavior also acts as suggestion.

CONTROL YOUR OWN MIRACLE MIND

Fortunately, you can change your mind purposefully and do yourself a great deal of good. You don't have to be a puppet, allowing your strings to be pulled by someone else. The battle for the mind has gone on since earliest history and when it has been conquered, it is drained of its contents and refilled with programming that serves the brain-washer.

The first step toward liberation from manipulation is to return your body to its rightful owner — yourself. Hypnosis can do that for you. In addition to being hypnotized by a therapist, you can also learn how to do it yourself. For most people who want to master "Self-Hypnosis," it helps to first experience the feeling with a trained technician. Group hypnosis is often the first step in that direction because there is comfort in sharing the experience with others, with similar problems to overcome.

It has long been known that visualization, without the addition of emotional desire, cannot bring about rapid results. That's why advertisers repeat their message over and over again, until it feels like an insult to human intelligence. By dulling the mind, commercials send hordes of viewers to the store to buy something they could probably be better, without.

Remote control seeps and creeps into the subconscious mind through a myriad of media sources. Beside television, there's radio, newspapers, magazines, computers, home videos and audio tapes; even the telephone with its increase of remote sales pitches.

Television and film are the most invasion of the lot; they not only reaches us through eyes and ears, but have powerful emotional impact because of the entertainment connection. Once we identitfy with a charcter on the screen we tend to imitate that behavior. The explosive growth of electronic communication has inflicted more harm on human behavior than help.

Conversely, the lighted screen could be a do-good savior. It could teach healthier way; it could build bridges between races and between nations; It could raise consciousness; help people understand each other and the world we live in. If these powerful devices where employed for the good of the people just imagine how rapid the improvement would be! Their hypnotic influence could be turned around to alleviate massive human suffering and degeneration. With the intelligent use of all of the human inventions for mind and behavior moderation, it could be done very quickly.

The next step in human evolution is to optimize the benefits of controlled thinking. At this point, most of us have been damaged by the intrusion of mental regulations that serve the interests of the few on top who control the means of communication. The manipulators design campaigns for enterprising merchandisers and millions of victims lose their free will. They begin with the youngest most impressionable minds; many later behavior problems are the result of a host of insidious, lifelong assaults on the brain.

The various techniques bring about debilitation, the breaking down of normal self-protective thought processes. The passivity of the viewer makes them easy prey to life threatening temptations, like self indulgent and useless products like candy, soft drinks, cigarettes, cake mixes, and a variety of beer products. Food products, especially candy, snacks and other deserts have resulted in childhood obesity which has serious repercussions on the left of self-esteem and social interaction.

The battle for control of the young mind has wide-ranging significance. Alcohol and smoking are portrayed in party scenes as signs of maturity. Jovial images, along with popular music, help sell the poison. Thus the acceptability of smoking becomes entrenched from the early years until the victim is trapped, forfeiting at least ten years of life.

Motivational analysts were called in by cigarette manufacturers who were getting bad press. Sales were slipping and Social Research became involved in solving the dilemma. Employing a group of psychiatrists who conducted a survey and declared that people continue to smoke because:

1.. It relieves mental and physical tension.

2.. It makes users feel carefree and sociable.

3.. It's satisfying after a sexual experience.

When they added up the results to this kind of advertising, sales picked up. The effort to get beneath the threshold of rational thinking, has even spread to subliminal messages that spin so fast they zip into the mind without our awareness. Alterations of thought patterns lead to changes in behavior. Victims who are not on guard are also influenced, not only by television advertising, but also by other people's opinions.

MAKE YOUR OWN MIRACLES HAPPEN

Fortunately, you can change your mind purposefully and do yourself a great deal of good. You don't have to be a puppet, allowing your behavioral strings to be pulled by manipulation. The battle for the mind has gone on since earliest history, and when conquered, it is drained of its contents and refilled with programming of the brain-washer.

The first step toward liberation is to return your mind and body to its rightful owner — yourself. Hypnosis can help you. In addition to being hypnotized by a therapist, you can also learn how to do it yourself or join a group. For most people who want to master self-hypnosis, it helps to first experience the feeling with a trained technician. Group hypnosis is also a first step in that direction because there is comfort in sharing the experience with others who have similar problems to overcome.

Whether you do it yourself or are helped by a professional, the hypnotic state is always an altered level of consciousness, the deepest of which is the therapeutic trance called CORE.

THERE'S MORE THAN JUST TELEVISION

Remote invasive conditioning seeps and creeps into the subconscious mind through a myriad of electronic sources. Beside television, there's radio, newspapers, magazines, computers, home videos and audio tapes; even the telephone and its sales pitches. Television and film are the most invasion of the lot; they not only reach us through eyes and ears, but have powerful emotional impact because of the entertainment factor.

Once we identify with a character on the screen we tend to imitate that behavior. Sources of information such as the Internet and television could use their hypnotic influence to alleviate massive human suffering and degeneration. With intelligent use of human invention, corrective therapy could be accomplished quickly. We'll never know what the human potential is, until we give our minds the opportunity to expand fully.

The next step in human evolution is to optimize the benefits of controlled thinking. At this point, most of us have been damaged by the intrusion of mental manipulation. They map campaigns for enterprising merchandisers while millions of victims lose their free will. Social scientists warn us of dire repercussions if the trend toward mind-control continues.

SERIOUS PROBLEMS LINKED TO MENTAL PROGRAMMING:

...Drug abuse has more than doubled in the last decade.

...Alcohol causes over 40% of relationship dysfunction.

...Sleep problems affect 60% of the American population

...Smoking is the greatest cause of death in the U.S.A.

...Eating disorders - Obesity, anorexia, bulimia, etc.

...Crimes against individuals and society as a whole.

...Domestic Violence, mental abuse and world conflict.

...Dissolution of family values as we've known them.

TV COUCH POTATOES - LONERS AND LOSERS

The media's advertisers play upon the anxieties of those who have given over their self-determination to the hidden persuaders. Heavy TV watchers tend to get out of shape in body and mind; as they obey the manipulator rather than motivate themselves to accomplish goals. As we listen to television and radio we are pummeled with suggestions to overindulge in starches, sugar, and all sorts of useless snacks.

For example, the American people consume twice as many baked goods as are good for the human body. Greed to succeed by exploiting others is threatening human health. It's time to use the human brain to overcome entrapment. Another danger is the inevitable isolation that too much television and computer fixation causes those who become addicted.

VIOLENCE APPLAUDED IN SPORTS

Weekends are a time for further conditioning viewer's minds with the violence of sports. There's a powerful lesson in discovering that brutality makes you a hero; all you have to do is win the game. Even "players" in sports are not really playing,

but serious about crushing their opponents. Proof of this is the innumerable lifelong injuries suffered by so many in the sports arena. In major league baseball, as well as football and hockey, physical fights are epidemic.

Often sportsmen sustain serious injuries. Yet, the rougher the game, the more they are admired as heroes by young people. Brutality is seen as play, causing kids to transfer roughhouse into their own playtime. Unfortunately, contact sports are often used as outlets for emotional problems, such as repressed anger.

Studies show when individuals become less competitive, they understand each other better, and their lives become more creative. Antagonism give way to empathy and rapport. Instead of striving to be better than another person, we can each enjoy becoming a better person than we were. Antagonisms can destroy our inner peace, without which we are prone to stress that can kill us in many ways.

We have seen an erosion of values in every way that we once deemed essential to rational living. Programs with violent content are at their worst when they involve police or friendly, good guys who use the same kind of violence as the bad guys. Imitating negative role models has led to more and more serious crimes committed by youth. Problem solving is equated with stabbing, shooting and beating rather than communication, compromise and reconciliation.

To raise adults that deal with others based on mutual consideration, we have to covert television from a destructive force to a helpful adjunct to parenting. Appreciation for another person's uniqueness and diversity could go a long way in correcting violence and crime, before it is indoctrinated into the character of the young. We see meanness and violence even in the cartoons designed for the very young preschooler.

Rage reactions to challenging situations are seen as acceptable. Domination and sadistic manipulation is common and admired as part of "a winning personality." It is no wonder that we grow up with confused values about what is appropriate in human relationships.

Solving human problems through violence and blood-letting has become part of almost every entertainment show. The chase, flight, fight and the inevitable shoot-out all teach cruel inhuman ways to settle disputes. There is rarely the choice of intelligent communication, reconciliation, or compromise. These are the values we should be teaching young people instead of settling disputes with fists, guns, knives and bombs. These instruments of stupidity are part of prime time shows, movie films and news reports.

When people are liberated to think for themselves, using introspection based on knowledge, they will be able to solve their personal problems, and the world's problems as well. When we follow mindlessly, we become something to serve the other's purpose and to that extent become less an authentic human and more of a mindless object.

GET TO KNOW YOUR NATURAL ASSETS

Instead of making oneself an object used by other people, self-hypnosis is very beneficial to authenticate oneself. It will help you discover your special uniqueness and ways of individual expression, which is innate in each of us.

Outside suggestion, when believed and accepted, becomes internalized. Once a suggestion is accepted and carried out by the subconscious, it begins its urging to be repeated and reinforced. Eventually what was once an outside suggestion becomes a habit of self-sabotage. Nowhere is this more evident than in the enormous amount of substances promoted in the media.

From infancy on, people have been told to expect panacea from one kind of pill, or another. This can translate into street drugs. Radio, newspapers, and television tell us to take a vast variety of pills to:

- Pep up...* Calm down
- Sleep at night...* Feel wide awake
- Correct Constipation...* Eliminate Diarrhea

People accept the television message for legal drugs and then take it even further, resorting to drugs which "blow their minds," (some lose their minds altogether).

There are over 10 million Americans taking legitimate drugs, since infancy. In addition, between 5 and 10 million people are addicted to drugs outside the law. The danger is clear. Much of what is supposed to pass for entertainment is not always in the best interests of the viewers.

SELLING THEIR POINT OF VIEW

In addition to substance inducement, race prejudice, violence, bad sexual behavior, and disturbed family interaction, have been displayed by a handful of giant monopolies with their own profit interests. They decide what people see, hear, eat and read; they select the priorities and form the mass-mind. What makes it more ominous is that politics tend to enforce this madness.

Commercial enterprise appears to take no responsibility or demonstrate ethical concern about the consequences of its actions. By the time a child reaches his/her teens, that child has been influenced by 10 to 15 thousand hours of violent behavior. Added to inappropriate programming are commercials which push products most families cannot afford. This is a contributing factor as to why many economically deprived young people resort to crime.

People, born since the advent of television, have had more interaction with the screen than with parents or teachers in schools. Many young people can no longer think for themselves. They just "talk the talk and walk the walk," whatever it is they see on TV.

When we assess how television, the most powerful of all the media, impacts on the brains of the recipient, we find that programs not only sell hair spray and deodorant, they sell a point of view. The images we watch and listen to, form our behavior and interaction with others. The industry is based upon engaging an audience and then delivering the mesmerized masses to advertisers, who wants their money.

MEDIA VALUES EXAMINED

Elizabeth Thoman founding editor of "Media Values Magazine" challenges the media and says: "Media no longer shape our culture; media have become our culture." She stresses the need to reverse negative programs to positive, calling for media literacy, to make the right choices and limit the time children spend before the screen. One of the most serious results is the damage to family relationships, since it demonstrates how disturbed people react in their lives. Rather than recycling obsolete stereotypes, we need to entertain with solutions.

YOUR MIND AND YOUR SELF-IMAGE

Every physical action is first seen in the mind's eye, where it can be accepted or rejected. This "yes and no" seesaw action is unending. Visual flashes take place on a subliminal level without conscious awareness. We reject, or accept a constant parade of possibilities. A silent commentary (inner self-talk) goes on deep within us whether to accept past influences or ignore them. Intelligence, the selector, picks the image and sends its report to the autonomic nervous system, which then triggers the physical action that must invariably follow. Even in talk-shows, people are so wired and hostile that they set the mood for angry confrontations rather than rational negotiation.

SHOCKING VIOLENT BEHAVIOR OF YOUTH

Children are more likely to model themselves upon what they see on film rather than what parents or teachers tell them is appropriate. The National Association for Better Broadcasting estimates that the average child sees physical damage done to about thirteen thousand people before the age of fifteen.

Other groups put the figure at almost double. One survey reported that 80 percent of the Saturday prime-time programs and half the characters on these shows committed some act of violence. Once they have been unconsciously hypnotized, they accept bloodshed as a solution to feeling powerless. Put into the hands of angry people, there are now approximately 75 million handguns being passed around illegally, in the United States.

TV PRESENTS OBSOLETE STEREOTYPES

Data compiled over many years by "The Cultural Indicators Project" in Philadelphia, revealed that prejudice is evident in the media against the elderly, women, African-Americans, Hispanics, Asians and other ethnic groups. In the United States acting out against those who are different from oneself, is considered permissible. Hate crimes come from prejudice towards people who do not conform to the defined norm in one's religion, race gender, or sexual orientation.

CHAPTER 5

VIOLENCE, CRIME AND PUNISHMENT

 Both Gangs and Cops Need Hypnosis
"Correctional" Prisons Don't Work

The gang population in the United States is over 1.5 million, (those are the ones we know about). Even some of the richest kids are ganging-up. Murder committed by children, continues to escalate, with over 3,000 victims reported in a single year. And that's just one aspect of the crime dilemma. A war is literally going on in many of our cities, including just a few blocks from the capitol in Washington, D.C., where crime, drug wars, and gang warfare are an every day concern.

As America staggers under the load of lawlessness and addiction, the underpinnings need to be examined. Despite surface concern and apprehension about where we are headed, as facts and figures grow more and more threatening, neither politicians nor health authorities are finding alternative solutions. It is because of this ineptitude on the part of people in power, that I am making the extravagant suggestion to initiate a vast program to counteract the negativity that young people have been subjected to.

We are not a fixed part of nature, but highly flexible with potentials of higher intelligent-spiritual ascendance, to exceed any yet known. Conventional methods, such as warehousing criminals, have not worked; two out of three will become repeat offenders.

A teenager, whom I was counseling, told me: "I wasn't wanted when I was born, but by the time I was fourteen, I was wanted in three states. When they caught me, I went to jail for two years. I felt like I was nothing before I went in, and even less when I got out." No one is born criminal; we are just born human, and if we don't receive guidance early in life we have to reach out for it later. Some people don't mature until they are middle aged or older. Maturity means discovering that the universe is neither for us nor against us. Nobody hands you happiness. You have to create it.

It is a symptom of our pressurized culture that many people strive too hard to live up to impossible standards and are often frustrated in the attempt. In our struggle to keep up with society's expectations, we over-strain our resources. Frustration is followed by exasperation, and hostility. When it converts to an accumulation of anger, people strike out in violent behavior.

WE NEED SOME DRASTIC CHANGES

The system of vengeance long sustained by the criminal justice system, has not reduced crime, but instead has made career criminals of disturbed young people. Jail time has not improved either the prisoner, or society. It costs 50,000 a year to keep a criminal in jail. Imagine how much could be done with that kind of money to develop talents and skills for a meaningful life. When inmates sit in cells with nothing to do but brood, you can't call it a correctional institution. Incarceration doesn't seem to help because the programs are inadequate.

To begin with, 70% of inmates are illiterate, having fallen through the cracks of our education system. They represent a significant slice of the 27 million Americans (one in five) who are considered functional illiterates. Fortunately, we can, with hypnosis training, teach most people to read and write. By so doing, we can lift their self-respect and help them feel part of normal society. Instead of resorting to brutality against others, or self-destructive habits, they can discover personal power.

THE NEED TO INSTILL MENTAL DISCIPLINE

Children with dangerous minds are roaming the school corridors. The proliferation of guns, knives, drugs and death in the school system, has spread out out of bounds and frightens all of us. Violence is rampant because no one has addressed the source of the rage brewing within young people who are struggling for self-empowerment.

Self-realization seldom happens spontaneously. We have been drilled, more or less, to be ashamed of self-praise, yet it's the only kind of appreciation that can re-mold our thinking about ourselves. Encouraging oneself by positive affirmation helps restore a sense of worth.

STAND TALL AND PROUD

Even the strongest among us finds it difficult to feel serene and secure in a world that is sorely troubled by mass tensions. People have to protect themselves because it isn't going to get any better, unless we make it better. The mounting stressful condition of the world is even more reason for aware people to have a personal method of remaining calm and objectively healthy in spite of it. Hypnosis will help you avoid being a victim of the environmental strait jacket.

While in your trance, critical judgment is set aside and your belief system becomes an ally. Your mind is like a vast, limitless garden. Suggestions are the seeds and hypnosis the soil that cultivates the seeds to blossom into beautiful thoughts that grow larger and stronger. Where there is an accumulation of weeds, or negative thoughts, we have to do some "mind cleaning" and root them out before good suggestions can flourish. As a result of dwelling on negative and self-debasing thinking, most people under estimate their potential and never reach their goals. A favorable mind-set is a necessary precursor to reconditioning or there will be subliminal resistance.

ARE YOU TIED TO YOUR PAST?

Only when you discard the chains that bind you, will you be ready to create a better future. This begins by making up your mind that you are master of your destiny. When you are unconscious of this power, you feel helpless and at the mercy of others. Your degree of anxiety and despair depends on what you do to change the course of your destiny. Otherwise life runs amuck and we continue to react like puppets. Humans can only have contentment when they take over the controls.

Sometimes it is necessary to compensate for the downgrading we may have been subjected to while growing up. Parental critical predictions are, in affect, suggestions that program their children's future. Criticism is only helpful if it is constructive and serves a good purpose.

Awareness of the past should not make you bitter. There is no point in castigating parents for mistakes. Ignorance about rearing children is universal and your parents were a natural part of that condition. Hypnosis can help you accept past conditioning without emotional trauma, knowing the effects are correctable.

REACHING OUT TO TROUBLED YOUTH

The entrenched system has failed both the teenage criminal and their victims, as well. Officials pay insufficient attention to troubled young people, until there is a crisis. Well, the crisis is NOW. Obsolete dogma is not working. Society has to demonstrate altruism, brotherly-sisterly love, mutual help, become the force that blows away the dark clouds of despair.

GANGS ATRRACT WEAKLINGS AND LOSERS

Gang joiners act like sheep, herded into a dangerous existence. Sheep let things happen to them, instead of shaping their own destiny. We all need to belong to something bigger and stronger than our individual selves. Gangs attract those who are fearful of life and overcome by problems. With self-empowerment they are able to face the same events as challenges. This is the basic difference between negative and positive thinking and happy living.

The first step toward achievement is to realize that improvement is possible. It's called "possibility thinking." Unless you think this way, you can be your own worst enemy, because hopelessness leads to desperate acts.

A TRUE SAD STORY

A thirteen year old told me, "The gang is my family. I owe my life to them." I failed to convince him to go to a shelter. He roamed the streets selling crack, until his head was cracked by a rival. His short life did not have to end that way. Society must offer supportive, practical, group solutions, especially to young people who grow up in a dysfunctional family, without proper role models. We need to guide them to connect what they feel; how it makes them think, with what they are doing because of the way they think and feel.

PROJECT AND ASSSERT YOUR RIGHTS

Getting what you want requires that you assert your needs. Having discovered what you want and that you are capable of achieving it, set about getting it as quickly as possible! You have to connect what you feel and think with what you are doing. With hypnosis you can erase your ineffective behavior and replace that mental space with more effective behavior.

NON-ASSERTIVE - ASSERTIVE - AGGRESSIVE

What is the difference between the three? The reason this is important is because success in life depends on choosing.

1... Non-Assertiveness is self-denial, a characteristic of a shy individual, too humble and easily victimized. Although this type of person does not speak up, they may release anger, later.

2... Assertiveness is a sign of honesty, strength, self-enhancing, self-respecting and open-minded. It shows confidence. Such a person is responsive to others and responsible to self.

3... Aggressiveness is selfish behavior at the expense of others. It is often forceful and can express hostility towards others. Gang leaders have this characteristic and often attract non-assertive people whom they can control.

How the others feel about you when you are:

1... Non-Assertive... Disdain, disrespect and superior.
2... Assertive... Respectful, trusting, and admired.
3... Aggressive... Hurt, diminished, angry, vengeful.

ASSERTIVENESS IS A LEARNED QUALITY

Few children are given the opportunity in their growing years to learn how to be assertive without being aggressive. Many grow up with deep feelings of insecurity, lack of confidence and loneliness. Self-alienation goes unrecognized by parents who are themselves non-assertive or too aggressive.

EXPRESS YOURSELF WITH CONVICTION

Your choice of words has unlimited power in both directions. If you express thoughts of a defeatist nature, you are surely going to be defeated. However, if you think and speak as a winner, you cannot help but act like a winner and win out over adversities. Your wondrous brain is constantly exercising control over both the involuntary and voluntary systems of your body. It determines all of its action based on recordings and memories of past experiences.

When you think like a loser, your brain presents all the old defeatist associations to further hamper you. There are also some helpful memories to recall if you really wish to do so. Everyone has both. Check and notice if you speak with enlightenment or are boxed into darkness.

Enlightenment gives us a clearer image of our future selves and goads us to further improvement. As our minds accept a new image we are encouraged to make the dream a reality. People need other people. Closeness to others helps us reach higher levels of mutual understanding. We need to break down the walls that separate people.

Today, about 60% of all families are dysfunctional, with marriages ending in divorce. Over 90% of all patients who see psychiatrists and psychoanalysts suffer from alienation and profound loneliness. Among young people suicide is a leading cause of death. During every day of the year, eighteen young people commit suicide. It is the second leading cause of death among American teenagers.

Over the years I have used hypnosis to help depressed people redesign themselves and discover their latent power. They have trained themselves to overcome obstacles, become more than anyone expected of them. Fear of adult responsibility, coupled with anxiety about the future, is cited as reasons for giving up on life.

There is the need to belong and share life's experiences with kindred souls. This is the primary way humans differ from other animals. We have emotions, sensitivities, and intelligence.

Young people who only feel secure in gang activities avoid revealing their true abilities to have one-on-one relationships. They shield themselves from possible failure in personal success. They block out the risk, as well as the reward, thus never fulfilling themselves.

We need to send this message to young people who are involved, "No matter how habitual the feeling of clan-comfort in "ganging up" has become, you can break the grip. You need not be forever dominated by them. You can, as many thousands of others have done, eliminate fear by using positive suggestion. Hypnosis will give you control over your impulses, as well as building increased confidence. Positive auto-suggestion will guide you toward acquiring greater gratification that comes from developing your own power. Don't blame circumstances — change them!

Instead of fear, you will see courage growing in your personality. You may not realize it at this moment, but, awake and asleep, you are constantly telling yourself things about yourself, both good and bad. What are you telling yourself about yourself? Is it based on some uninformed source? You will be helped in sharing group hypnotherapy because it is the highest form of communicative intimacy.

In working with young people who have been in and out of prisons, I realized that there is an emotional state that goes with the risk-taking activity of breaking the law. The adrenaline rush is described this way: "I feel my heart pounding; my palms are wet and clammy; I feel a gnawing, tense sensation in my stomach; it's like something terrible is going to happen and it usually does — I usually get caught."

HYPNOSIS USED IN HAWAII STATE PRISONS

A news report published by the National Board for Hypnotherapy calls attention to the successful work being done with hypnosis in stress management programs. The Hawaii State Prison System has recognized that recidivism can be the result of addictive behavior. Because life outside the prison system may be difficult after having been programmed to the life inside, repeat offenders may be drawn to repeat a crime.

There is also the factor of the excitement of capture, the energy rush and the release of endorphins, which often occur during commission of a crime. In addition to therapy sessions inside the facility, when inmates are released from Hawaii State Prisons they receive free hypnotherapy sessions.

Prison officials negotiate lifestyle plans for those prisoners who have to adjust to freedom. Each person receives three hours of therapy where they are taught self-hypnosis for self-esteem and personal success. A repeat offender had this to say about the help he received from hypnosis: "It has opened my mind to changing for the better. I am open to new things. I'm curious about everything there is to learn. I'm going to make my mark in some way. I will never be behind bars again."

The prison system is planning to add addiction hypnotherapy to their already funded, general cognitive treatment program. This is a beacon light which can act as a role model for police systems in other states, and, hopefully, will radiate out to the rest of the world.

POLICE ARE ALSO VICTIMS OF CRIME

In California, Joshua Blyden, hypnotist and former firearms instructor for the police force has created an outline for a special hypnosis program to help reduce the enormous stress facing law enforcement officers.

"Law Enforcement Augmentation Program" (LEAP)

With the increase in crime in the United States and early release and parole of convicted criminals, the police officer on the street has, by virtue of circumstances beyond his/her control, been forced to contend with stress factors that have become significantly higher in recent years. The rookie police officer is required to cope with rapes, murders, robberies, gang warfare, drug dealers and a sometimes indifferent public as well as a "revolving door Justice system".

The list is endless. Violence in the streets has increased several fold from thirty years ago. While most law enforcement agencies offer staff psychologists and psychiatrists with an "open door policy," more often than not, the damage has already been done to the officer. Too little, too late. This is not to say that health professionals are not doing an outstanding job in helping the officers in question; they are.

Police are human beings, not emotionless robots, and as such they cannot help being affected by all the trauma going on around them, in the streets, and in their own personal lives, as a result of the stress they are expected to endure. Fortunately, there is a solution.

The time has come to infuse a program of hypnosis into existing police academy education, with concurrent instruction in self-hypnosis training. This program when implemented will empower Law Enforcement trainees to enhance their fortitude, emotional stability and curtail alcohol use, drug tendencies and attrition.

A survey was conducted with the co-operation of 103 sworn police officers to obtain a ranking of stressors unique to their line of work. The selection was randomized from the general population in a specific geographical area. Surveys were sent by interdepartmental mail, with a response rate of 93%. Officers responding to the survey represented a cross variety of experience, age, rank and ethnic backgrounds.

Officers ranked work stressors on the 60-item Police Stress Survey developed by Speilberger, Westberry, Grier and Greenfield (1981). Officers responded to individual items on a scale of 0-100. The number 0 having the least value or "no stress" and 100 representing the "maximum stress."

Table 1 gives the officers' ratings of stressors. Mean scores ranged from a low of 22.5 (racial conflicts) to a high of 79.4 (killing in the line of duty). The two top-ranked stress factors were:

1. Killing in the line of duty (M = 79.4).

2. Experiencing a fellow officer killed (M = 76.7).

3. Organizational/administrative. Shift work was ranked as the highest organizational stressor (M = 61.2)

4. inadequate departmental support (M = 60.9).

STRESS AREAS TO BE COVERED BY HYPNOSIS:

a.   Organizational/administrative/departmental
b.   Inherent/response to calls/death of fellow officer
c.   Stress due to personal/family/friends, etc.
d.   Increase learning/memory/concentration/recall
e.   Increase skills/shooting/tactics/communication
f.   Instruction in auto-hypnosis and life skills

The program is designed to accommodate police cadets upon their entry into any given law enforcement academy in the United States. While there are other countries that could benefit from the program, the pilot procedure should be done in the U.S. and preferably conducted within a small police department training facility.

Conducting the program in such a fashion would enable tighter system control, allowing closer monitoring and performance verification of the initial test subjects.

1. Establish facts pertaining to:

a. Stress, Physical & Psychological

b. Alcoholism abuse rate

c. Drug abuse rate

d. Spouse abuse rate

e. Suicide rate

Police Stressors by Mean Scores on Survey:

Killing someone in the line of duty............ **79.4**
Physical attack on self............................ **71.0**
Battered child...................................... **69.2**
High-speed chases................................. **63.7**
Accident in patrol car........................... **59.9**
Excessive discipline.............................. **53.3**
Death notifications............................... **52.6**
Family disputes................................... **52.0**
Lack of recognition............................... **48.1**
Physical injury on job........................... **47.1**
Excessive paperwork............................. **43.2**
Public criticism................................... **39.5**
Personal insult from citizen.................... **36.7**
Promotion competition.......................... **29.5**
Racial conflicts................................... **22.5**

ANGER MANAGEMENT PROGRAM

More and more people accept uncontrolled anger as normal. Seeking to survive by competitive standards has driven a wedge between our true selves and the expectation of the social system we exist in. Even "players" in sports like football, are not really playing, but serious about crushing their opponents. Proof of this is the innumerable lifelong injuries suffered by so many.

In major league baseball, as well as football and hockey, physical fights have become epidemic. Often sportsmen sustain serious injuries that take them out of action. Among football players the average life-span rarely exceeds sixty. Yet, the rougher they behave, the more they are admired as heroes by their fans, many of whom are impressionable children.

Brutality is seen as entertainment and emulated in the random roughhouse in some children's playtime. Studies show that as individuals become less aggressive, they understand each other better and their lives become more creative and interesting. Antagonism can give way to empathy and rapport with mental training. Instead of striving to be better than another person, we can each become a better person than we are, and relate with kindness to one another.

Competition, when it involves putting down another person and gaining financial reward has an element of cruelty. It stands in the way of our natural need for communication with others based on sharing and caring, rather than demoting the other's abilities. Antagonisms can destroy our inner peace without which we are prone to stress that can ill us in a myriad of ways.

Television programs with violent content are at their worst when they involve police or friendly good guys who use the same kind of mindless violence to conquer and brutalize the bad guys. Imitating negative role models has led to more and more serious crimes committed by children. Problem solving is being equated with stabbing, shooting and beating rather than communication, compromise and reconciliation.

KINDNESS NEEDS TO BE TAUGHT

To raise adults that deal with others based on kindness and consideration, we have to convert television from a destructive force to a helpful adjunct to parenting. Appreciation for another person's uniqueness and diversity goes a long way in correcting violence and crime before it is indoctrinated into the character of the young. We see meanness and violence even in the cartoons designed for preschooler.

Rage reactions to challenging situations are seen as acceptable. Domination and sadistic manipulation is common and admired as part of "a winning personality." It is no wonder that children grow up to be adults who have confused values about what is right and wrong. The dogma of "Dog eat dog...the survival of the fittest" hasn't worked for happines for the greatest number of people.

Data compiled over many years by "The Cultural Indicators Project" in Philadelphia, revealed that much of crime results from prejudice against a particular segment of people. This is evident in violence against women, the elderly, children, African-Americans, Hispanics, Asians and other ethnic groups.

In the United States, acting out against those who are different from oneself, is often overlooked. Hate crimes come from prejudice towards a group of people who do not conform to the defined norm in one's own religion, race gender, or sexual orientation. It is nourished by a societal system of sub-rosa discrimination due to racism, sexism and anti-semitism. This issue is seldom addressed on television programs.

POVERTY IS NOT STUPIDITY

In addition, we often see in moves and on television programs, images of the poor and powerless depicted as ignorant, but also lacking in intelligence. The more hours people watch, the less likely they are to be open to people of different backgrounds. The three greatest sins are:

1. Denying another person's equal rights.

2. Sabotaging fulfillment of one's potential.

3. Avoiding responsibility for one's actions.

Motivation developed with hypnosis, can spur you to improve by leaps and bounds. Motivation is what makes a person practice with regularity. It is only consistent, highly motivated practice of a system of reconditioning such as detailed here that can change a person into one who is capable of living life to the fullest.

CHAPTER **6**

GROUP TRAINING FOR SELF-IMPROVEMENT

<u>Reprogramming Anti-Social Behavior</u>
<u>Building Self-Esteem and Confidence</u>

We need a social system, with community support, based on radically altered sensibilities, where we each care about the other person. Hypnosis methods can be applied on a one-to-one basis, or in group training, which minimizes cost. Also, as individuals master the technique, they are then prepared to tutor beginners. Each graduate becomes a mentor for the next person to enter the group. This is necessary because there is so much to be done, so many issues that threaten the lives of millions of people.

Those who are economically and emotionally secure need to demonstrate altruism, brotherly-sisterly love, become part of the force that blows away the dark clouds of despair and helps build a new kind of humanity. Hypnosis is effective because it combines the three pillars of cultural progress:

1... **Philosophical** - Hypnosis promotes a great depth of thoughtfulness, with inner composure, and acts as a guide to investigate what the truth is bout being human.

2... **Scientific** - Hypnosis works on a dependable principle of mind-altering, which has been replicated in random samplings of people, anywhere in the world.

3... **Creative** - Expressed in visualizations during guided imagery, hypnosis releases innate talents and skills that have been dormant in the individual.

It has long been known that imagination, without a philosophy and scientific application, may remain in the realm of wishful-thinking.

GROUP HYPNOSIS RAPIDLY CORRECTS MASS PROBLEMS.

We can change ourselves and the world in just one generation if we use the knowledge of self-empowerment which is within each of us. Emergency methods need to be used if we are to avoid the rapid decline of the human species. Addiction and other stress-related problems are so prevalent and pervasive that time is of the essence.

Because there are not enough skilled hypnotists to work on a one-to-one basis, grouping together becomes the most viable method of correction. People need other people, and this is as true for young people as it is for older people. Sharing empathy helps us to grow to higher levels of awareness that we are all more alike than we are different.

Countless walls separate people, both literally and figuratively. This makes it difficult for them to communicate in order to work out their mutual needs. Real self-knowledge can only be gained through the interaction between people.

Setting up self-healing groups is quite simple. Almost everyone in our society lives and works in some kind of organizations — schools, hospitals, prisons, drug rehab centers, and shelters for the homeless and abused. Community centers will find it is possible to help people with the least expense. One hypnotic facilitator can train hundreds of people in a week. I have conducted therapy in group, for the past twenty years, whenever my private practice permitted it.

I have found there are three kinds of people:

1. Those that make things happen (Strong minded individuals)
2. Those that watch things happen (Go along as followers)
3. Those that ask: what's happening? (Because they don't think)

SOME PROBLEMS THAT RESPOND TO GROUP HYPNOSIS:

1... Eating disorders such as obesity, anorexia, bulimia, special diets such as diabetes and elevated cholesterol. Obesity which leads the list, is a health problem for one out of three American women and one out of four men. Poor people are among the fattest, due to ignorance about proper nutrition. Expensive weight loss systems are not available to them.

2... Addictive behavior such as alcoholism, reckless driving, drug abuse, smoking, uppers, lowers and pain killers. Alcohol and drugs disturb the brain's sensitive reactors, becloud memory and sequential thinking. The hypnosis student learns to self-limit, to confine and control compulsive urges.

3... Domestic Violence, molestation of children and cruelty to the elderly. People who maim and kill can be converted to peaceful people. Also, there are 26 million veterans of various wars living useless lives that need help in self-fulfillment.

4... Learning abilities maximized. Illiteracy can be abolished, languages learned quickly, and job training facilitated. Most people have barely tapped their potential.

5... Crime control and rehabilitation of our prison system by preparing inmates to lead a new and better life when they leave. Boot camps can be provided for youth training for jobs when they are released. Aftercare workshops can provide therapists to teach self-empowerment. We should stop the nonsense of building more prisons; instead put the money into hypnotic training of skills and provide meaningful work programs. Millions are wasted on prisons warehousing criminals who should have been taught social responsibility in the first place.

6... Enabling the handicapped and wheel-chair bound, by training them to optimize natural skills and talents so they can be gainfully employed. Raising self-esteem by the social interaction of people who have been limited socially because they are living as "shut-ins."

7... Retarding the aging process with time regression. Subliminal persuasion to abide by healthy behavior to extend mind and body function. Group hypnosis abolishes anxiety and fear of abandonment and dying. Empathy is shared and hope escalates.

8... Phobias and irrational fears can be assuaged for millions of people who feel panic about heights, flying, crime and scores of other inbred anxieties. An expectant thought always precedes a phobic reaction because the brain is linked to the nervous system. Changing requires taking charge of the irrational impulse by getting inside your mind and mastering it. That's the best way to manage your irrational emotions.

9... Concentration and memory recall will improve from entering one's CORE (Center Of Radiant Energy). Optimum mind-control and focus are enhanced, and creative invention. Plan your life and live your plan.

10...Improving intimacy for couples involves breaking down inhibitions and developing mental mastery over sensual responses. Saving the family unit by eliminating infidelity and promiscuity.

11...Teen pregnancy has increased seventy percent in the last decade. We give teenage girls mixed messages — to look sexy like the girls o television, while at the same time, abstain from sexual activity. We need group classes to teach sexual anatomy and social values — this can take place in conjunction with group hypnosis training.

An immediate challenge is to probe the connection between brain, emotions, and the sudden surge of sexual hormones in the young adult. How this process affects behavior is an important area to discuss with teenagers.

EMPOWERING THE GROUP

Group therapy enables the unable to become able by sharing experiences of others in similar straits. For example, in the area of education a coalition of various groups such as students, teachers, parents and community organizations set up programs facilitated by a trained hypnotist. We can make winners out of people who see themselves as losers.

The group can be hypnotized as a whole, ranging from about ten people to several hundred. I have hypnotized several thousand people at a huge sales rally and judging by the show of hands 80 percent where able to follow the procedure and believe they "went under." Whether you do it yourself, or are helped by a professional, in group or solo, the hypnotic state is reached through altering your concentration.

Once the trance level is achieved, suggestions are fed to your receptive mind to accomplish whatever you choose as your program of improvement.

In discussing this subject with my colleagues, the inevitable question arises: Who decides who gets hypnotized, and for what purpose? The answer is simple —

The person who needs help makes all the decisions and is always in control. Without each individual's active participation, the results could be disappointing. A person will not accept suggestion unless he has agreed to its application.

The group can be hypnotized as a whole, ranging from about ten people to several hundred. I have hypnotized several thousand people at a huge sales rally and judging by the show of hands about 80 percent where able to follow the procedure and believe they went into some level of trance. Group suggestion is very successful, because the individuals share the same problem. This empathy has a contagious reaction on each participants as they identify with each others problems.

GROUP PARTICIPANTS FOLLOW THESE STEPS:

1. **Pre-Induction** - Participants discuss their physical and emotional problems; their degree of self esteem; self-confidence; the type of relationships they've have been involved in; attitudes; abilities; and inner-qualities. This procedure provides the participants with awareness of their goals.

2. **Standard Induction** - Although many special types of methods are available, our experience indicates that the most appropriate induction is the one least threatening for beginners. This is called "The Progressive Relaxation Technique." This method instructs subjects to focus and relax different parts of their bodies, until they are totally free of physical tension.

3. **Deepening Techniques** - The facilitators have various techniques to chose from. The purpose here is to take the subjects into deep hypnosis. Contrary to "one-on-one" office hypnotherapy where depth is not always essential to good results, the greater the depth in group induction, the greater the sense of participation among the newcomers.

4. **Self Analysis** - While going through the hypnotic experience, participants are asked guiding questions that will allow them to become intimately familiar with their mind's ability to recall the roots of their problems. They can be given a pad and pen to write their answers, for later discussion.

5. Visualizing the Solution - This varies depending on the problem, addiction or specific needs of each person. They are given choices of images to focus upon, such as skill in sports, looking slimmer, sobriety, success on a job, etc...

6. Coming Out Of The Trance - The participants share their experience and encourage each other for future group sessions.

ABOUT GROUP COOPERATION

Here's a great 'Goose Story' about group effort. When geese head south for the winter, they fly in a 'V' formation and in this way they help each other get to their mutual destination. Each bird flaps its wings to create an up-lift, a boost, for the bird immediately following. This 'V' formation adds over 70 percent greater flying range than if each bird flew on its own.

Similarly, people who share a common purpose and sense of community can get where they are going easier when they combine their efforts. Applying good goose sense, we should cooperate with those who are headed toward the same goals we are. Another thing humans can learn is that geese 'honk' encouragement to those up front to keep up their speed and to show that the efforts of the followers are appreciated. We may have greater intelligence, but geese seem to make more sense.

GROUP HYPNOSIS IS NOT STAGE HYPNOSIS

Stage hypnotists command: "You will do as I say!" This has outlived it's usefulness in an era of self-empowerment. It has taken a century to alleviate the impression made upon millions of people by stage hypnotists who often suggested demeaning behavior to amuse the audience. Domineering hypnotists demand obedience, rather than inquiring as to what's best for the subject.

HOW TO LEAD A GROUP INDUCTION

This varies depending upon the type of people in the group. The orientation to empowerment is given in simple language, allowing ample time for response. When I've worked with young people who are in trouble with the law, I have started out by saying:

"You must choose whether you wish to perpetuate a troubled life, with low self-esteem and anti-social attitude or whether you are ready to be respected for your abilities and decency. If you want to be somebody people look up to instead down at, there is nothing to stand in your way but yourself. Every time you think and every time you speak, you should know that each one of your thoughts and words brings with it a reaction from other people. How you succeed in life depends on the way you affect other people. You can change for the better, by changing your mind about yourself.

CREATING A PERSONAL PROGRAM

After the introduction, I begin by giving each person a card or slip of paper on which they list the number one problem that they share with the rest of the group; in addition, a personal problem that he/she wishes to correct. In this way, self-involvement is established and cooperation is assured. Later, after I complete the mass suggestion, when they are still in an altered state (hypnotized), I will ask them to focus on one of their personal problems. This technique increases motivation and greater acceptance of the mass problem.

QUESTIONS ANSWERED BEFORE INDUCTION

There are usually questions about how hypnosis works and the leader must answer the myths and misconceptions before there is a sense of security in relaxing and accepting suggestion. Some typical questions are:

Q... Are there some people who cannot be hypnotized?

A... Only those people who's intelligence is below normal because they have difficulty understanding the process. I'm sure nobody here has that problem.

Q... Could a hypnotist put me under and make me do something I don't want to?

A... No. You always have a watchful mind and will awaken and refuse to take suggestion which goes against your beliefs.

Q... What is the difference between being hypnotized and doing self-hypnosis?

A... Some people need to experience the altered state with outside direction before they know what to expect. Once they do, it is easier to do it themselves.

Q... What makes hypnosis work, the relaxation or the power of positive suggestion?

A... Both. The relaxation helps you drift into an altered state of mind where you visualize the improvement and the suggestion plants the seeds into your subconscious mind.

Q... What's the difference between transcendental meditation and hypnosis?

A... Meditation is useful for relaxing and detaching one's mind and emotions

from stress, while hypnosis dissolves the stress rather than transcend it.

Q...What is the difference between psychology and the practice of hypnosis?

A...Whereas psychology is the study of human behavior, (cause and effect); hypnosis is the catalyst to change unwanted behavior.

Hypnosis is an altered state of consciousness, allowing access to the highly suggestible subconscious. This is accomplished by quieting the conscious mind and setting aside anxiety. Research informs us that electrical changes take place in the brain during hypnosis that alter the rhythms of your brain waves. Brain waves are changed from the waking state "Beta" to a slower, deeper beat called "Theta."

CHECK YOURSELF OUT

To accomplish their aims, each person will receives a "Check-List" to help them identify, and then select their problems, which they write down on a card. They number each issue in relation to its priority. Here are a few of the choices possible:

1. LEARN TO READ AND WRITE BETTER

2. BUILD SELF-ESTEEM AND CONFIDENCE

3. DEVELOP TALENTS AND NEW SKILLS

4. STOP SMOKING NOW...LOSE THE URGE.

5. PERMANENT WEIGHT LOSS — STICK TO DIET

6. IMPROVE THE IMMUNE SYSTEM BY BEHAVIOR

7. ENERGY...EXCEL AT CHOSEN SPORT

8. CORRECT INSOMNIA...SLEEP THROUGH THE NIGHT.

9. WIN RESPECT FROM OTHER PEOPLE

After the members of the group have made their selections, they are relaxed and inducted into the trance level. They are now receptive to suggestion and ready for the following procedure. While there are many group problems, I will demonstrate smoking cessation an example:

SCRIPT FOR GROUP LEADERS ON SMOKING

This is the imagery that follows the basic relaxation and induction, after breathing regulation and eye closure. Hypnotist: "See yourself strolling in the country on a beautiful day, the sun is shining and all is right with the world. You look up into the trees and you see a bird singing. It's round chest is puffed out as it breathes the clean air. You are aware of the air that you share with all life on this planet. Just as you would not blow smoke into the face of a bird, a kitten, or a child, so you do not blow smoke into yourself. You are a valuable human being and have self-respect". Give yourself the following suggestions as I speak them aloud, say to yourself, silently:

"With each breath I breathe I am contented and satisfied. Other smokers will have no influence or tempt me to weaken. Each time the thought of a cigarette occurs to me, instead of lighting up I will raise my arms over head and take a deep breath of clean air."

In spite of the Surgeon General's warning: "Smoking causes lung cancer, heart disease, emphysema and may complicate pregnancy," millions of addicted people remain entrapped.

Patrick Reynolds, grandson of the founder of one of the world's largest tobacco companies, has disowned the family business and is urging people to kick the deadly habit. In an interview on television, he described the gruesome death from emphysema of both his father and brother who were heavy smokers. At that point he himself quit smoking, and is now a staunch spokesperson for putting the nasty business out of business. Of equally destructive influence is alcoholism which responds well in group therapy with all levels of hypnosis. However, a light trance requires more sessions.

ALCOHOL — A MIND-ALTERING DRUG

Alcoholism has broken up more families than infidelity. It alters moods, and causes changes in the body and brain. Alcohol is a "downer," because it depresses the central nervous system. This can cause slurred speech, passing out, loss of memory and premature aging. In addition, the medical consequences are horrendous, everything from cancer to deadly heart disease. Why do people drink? They say to forget their worries, pains, stress. They say it helps them overcome a sense of failure. The truth is, it does the opposite. Alcohol is the number one cause of premature death, due to its weakening of the immune system.

MIND-BODY HEALING GROUPS

The trend toward using the hypnotic trance for group healing has already begun, and is bringing outstanding results. In a survey conducted at a meeting of the American Academy of Physicians, 99% said they were convinced that belief can heal. Dr. Herbert Benson said, "We've seen that belief is powerful in conditions including angina pectoris, asthma, duodenal ulcers, congestive heart failure, diabetes, and various forms of pain."

World-class medical centers like the University of California in Los Angeles, have included hypnosis training in their healthcare programs. They call their group "Hypnosis and Mind-Body Medicine." A psychologist-hypnotist leads the group where they discuss how hypnosis is used to affect healing, modify physical symptoms and promote well-being. Hypnosis is appreciated by patients because it produces the most effective results in the shortest time.

There are a number of hypnotherapy group going on around this country, which concentrate on helping the A.I.D.S. victims. The experimental use of hypnotism in controlling the virus is generating some promising results. Participants report a noticeable reduction in anxiety; sleep improvement; greater energy; better concentration and most important — greater hope for recovery.

CHILDBIRTHING GROUP

Groups which feature hypnotic techniques, such as breathing release, differential relaxation, and pain reduction are springing up in many large cities. Every expectant mom should have the opportunity to take part in a hypnosis training group. She would discover that delivery does not have to be as painful as most pregnant women fear. The support people, such as husbands, lovers and friends, also attend and learn hypnosis techniques. Hypnosis has been found useful for assuring good results in healthy mother's for the nursing infant.

AFFIRMATIVE ATTITUDE IS BASIC TO HEALTH

A steady, firm stand is needed before one can move forward without tottering.

Hypnosis trained minds can resist negativism with steadfastness. The average person's thinking is cluttered with blocks of apathy, skepticism, and fears. Fears will always try to rear their ugly heads and must be slapped down with vigor. Only the zealous and determined ever succeed in changing for the better.

The only worthwhile thing to learn from the past is how to avoid repeating the same mistakes over again. Mistakes are part of life's experiences, and the only person who never makes a mistake is the one who never attempts anything. Stewing in old juices of despair only serves to seep them deeper into the flesh of our souls. Misinformation does not have to be a permanent disaster.

CONVERT GANGS INTO GROUP THERAPY

A study from Iowa State University suggests that venting rage fails to relieve hostility. The best way to lessen an emotional crisis is to see yourself as capable of negotiation to a fair resolution. You should know that angry thoughts can disturb your glandular system, your nerves, and digestive organs.

Another area for group hypnosis is helping members of youth gangs to discover they have a brain, and that they can become independent and powerful. Insecurity and anger form the foundation for attracting young people to gang life. Here we have already existing groups that can be helped to explore their talents. An improved image builds confident expectations that can turn the tide from merely wanting a decent life to actually living one.

In his own inimitable way, Shakespeare summed up the virtues of positive autosuggestion in the following way: "Assume a virtue, if you have it not." He stated poetically what is known to be a basic science of the mind. Thoughts reach out and move us to overcome shortcomings, if they are constructive rather than destructive.

We feel good about ourselves to the degree that we are in control of our actions. When we are out of control, we become victims of retaliation. We are responsible when we create circumstances, like associating with troublesome people or using substances like drugs, etc.

If you believe in yourself, you become your own best friend, because we are all greatly influenced by our own inner voice. What you say to yourself unconsciously today, affects what you do tomorrow.

Where do the negative thoughts come from? Thinking and the action that follows can be likened to a tree. Just as much substance is invisible as is showing above the surface. Our branches are only the projection of the kind of roots that nourish them. Unfortunately, the vast majority of people engage in activities without the slightest idea of the depth of their subconscious minds.

Albert Einstein said, "Imagination is more powerful than knowledge." Through visualization, you can discover what you want and that you are capable of attaining it with the power of the mind. We are all creative to some degree.

BECOME A CREATIVE PERSON

While we cannot expect a problem-free life, we can learn how to accept problems as challenges and use our mental power to do something constructive about it. We only learn by doing. There are only two types of people who will not be able to benefit from hypnosis training:

1. Those who are intellectually incapable of understanding.

2. Those who are unwilling to improve because they feel unworthy.

HOW IT FELT THE FIRST TIME

Here are some definitions and endorsements from people who have participated in group hypnosis for various improvement purposes. They say this about hypnosis:

"A natural state of mind, an inner space of detached spiritual serenity The calmness stays afterwards and makes you aware of your power to ignore food you don't need."

"Hypnosis gives you the ability to direct your mental energy into a special area. I used it to visualize my body the way I wanted it to be, healthier and younger. My vision became my reality, because I started to exercise and watched what I was eating."

"I was very stressed out. Hypnosis gave me terrific relaxation and improved my sleep. Also, for the first time in my life, I am sleeping through the night and waking up with energy, which has always been a problem with me."

"Hypnosis gave me the confidence to quit using uppers and downers and other drugs I wont mention. It directed my mind away from food as a source of satisfaction. Instead I use my natural resources."

"For me, going into hypnosis has protected me from losing control around certain people, who in the past pushed me into arguments and fights. Now I know how to handle the anger, without losing my temper over little things that don't matter."

"I felt as if I was in a really nice dream, where I could see the way I wanted my life to be. I could visualize how much better I would be if I got out on my own without having to belong to a gang."

CHAPTER 7

SUCCESS BY OVERCOMING OBSTACLES

<u>Plan Your Work - Work Your Plan</u>
<u>Motivation Not Procrastination</u>

What are you doing with your one wonderful life? You must choose whether you waste it, or embrace it fully. If the latter is true, there is nothing to stand in your way, but yourself. Hypnosis will help you because it acts as catalyst to break the cords that keep us tied to mediocrity. It helps us to persevere in the face of adversity. Success only comes to those who have the courage to change and are willing to investigate new avenues.

Most people fear failure; others fear success, because with success comes responsibility. How do you stop the self-defeating cycle? Try this: Think of how success would feel, and you will begin to feel the way you think.

<u>POSITIVE SUGGESTIONS TO SUCCESS</u>

Auto-suggestions are self-commands. If they start the mind and body moving in the right direction, they are the right kind of suggestions. Good thoughts are activators which bring about affirmative improvements. Not only are self-suggestions self-commands, they build self-esteem, self-confidence, and self-love. To reach this high level, we must be constantly on guard against verbal and non-verbal put-downs, by others and self.

Remember, all outside suggestion, past and present, is transformed into self-suggestion by one's failure to reject. If you desire to be more than a puppet in life, you must carefully examine other people's expressions before making them your own. Like a computer, you can program your mind to properly activate your life and reach wanted goals. However, the output can only be as good as the input.

What are you putting into your mind? All the good that can come to you in your lifetime must come through your own brain. Hypnosis guides us out of "Never-Never Land" into a place where possibility-thinking brings positive rewards.

MOTIVATION FUELS YOUR DRIVE

In order to stop pushing the door marked pull, and move up the rungs of our potential ladder, dogged persistence is necessary. We are always making subconscious choices between success and failure. What are you telling yourself about yourself? Listen to the way that you describe yourself to others. Do you build yourself up or put yourself down?

Once you consciously turn your mental wheels in the right direction, they will quickly propel you toward your goal. Suggestion can create a loser. but the right suggestion can turn the loser into a winner. Feeling like a loser happens on an unaware level; it creeps up on people during times of stress. However, once your thinking is oriented toward a specific goal, things begin to happen, sometimes in a subtle way, sometimes quite dramatically, depending on your dedication. Temporary setbacks will not disturb you because you will weigh all the evidence rationally, and move onward and upward.

MAKE A COMMITMENT TO YOURSELF

You cannot succeed at anything if your mind expects failure. It would seem, at first thought, that any man or woman would prefer to be successful. Yet, this is not so. Many otherwise normal people subconsciously anticipate failure and by so doing, sabotage themselves. One of the tragedies of life is that so many people spend their lives without even knowing that their thoughts are interfering with their degree of success.

With hypnotic programming, temporary setbacks will not disturb you because you will weigh the evidence rationally and know that you are following a program that must lead you to your goal. Instead of avoiding challenges, welcome every opportunity to explore your abilities. Once you have committed yourself to a goal, all the loose pieces begin to fall into place. Decision assures realization; flooding the mind with hopeful anticipation.

Hypnosis puts you in the driver's seat of your life instead of being a passenger on someone else's success trip. It helps you avoid the pot holes and strengthens you to stay on course. Once your thinking is oriented toward a specific goal, things begin to happen, sometimes in a subtle way, sometimes quite dramatically, depending on your dedication.

A steady, firm stand is needed before one can move forward without tottering. We must face up to the contrariness within our habit-trained minds and resist negativism with courage and steadfastness. The average person's thinking is cluttered with blocks of apathy, skepticism, and fear. Fear will always try to rear its ugly heads and must be slapped down with vigor. Only the determined ever succeed in changing for the better.

Keep in mind that motivation can spur you to improve by leaps and bounds. Motivation is what makes a person practice with regularity. It is only consistent practice of reconditioning such as detailed here that can change an individual with problems into a person capable of living life to the fullest.

YOUR MIND IS A RECORDER

Everything you hear and think is impressed into the crevices of your brain. Fortunately, you can erase what is no longer useful and replace the space with better information. Hang-ups and inhibitions can be alleviated, even wiped out, if motivation is strong enough. Get ready to paint a new self-portrait that does yourself justice. Painful emotions twist the picture like a reflection in a distorted mirror. Clearing up this mottled reflection takes practiced reconditioning through deep hypnosis.

When you gain control by training your mind, it will subconsciously direct you toward your goals. You can do incredible things when you learn to use your brain as a problem-solver. Your brain is a fantastic instrument for change. If we built a computer with the power of your brain, that computer would have to be as big as the Empire State Building. And still, it would not have the magic of human imagination.

THINK AND SPEAK LIKE A WINNER

Suggestion has unlimited power to move you in any direction. If your thoughts are of a defeatist nature, you are surely going to be defeated. However, if you think and speak as a winner, you cannot help but act like one and win out over adversities. Your wondrous brain is constantly exercising control over both the involuntary and voluntary systems of your body. It determines all of its action based on memories of past suggestion and early training. Everyone has some helpful memories to recall, as well as troublesome ones. Check it out. Notice what you are telling yourself, about yourself.

OPTIMIZING SKILLS AND TALENTS

There is no limit to what your mind can conjure up to spur latent abilities and kindle the flame of creativity. You can picture fulfillment and self-mastery without which success is impossible. Hypnosis enlarges upon the mundane and escalates talent and paves the way for rapid learning.

Every physical action is first seen in the mind's eye, where it is accepted or rejected. This "yes and no" seesaw is unending. You may not be aware this is taking place because it happens very quickly. These flashes take place on a subliminal level without involving normal awareness. We view, screen, reject, or accept a constant parade of past events. A silent commentary goes on within whether to be influenced by them or toss them aside. Intelligence selects the image and sends its report to the conscious mind.

Ask yourself: "What am I telling myself about myself? Is it helping or hindering me?" If what you are saying is less than affirmative, then you are probably not living up to your potential. Almost everyone is susceptible to the scientific process of change.

We are constantly bombarded by suggestions that serve someone else's purpose instead of our own. Begin to protect yourself. When an idea is presented to you, listen with a third ear to its subtle nuances. Consider from where it came and why it was projected. If you think it may be contrary to your best interests, reject it immediately. There are many avenues of suggestion that influence success:

- What people tell us about ourselves
- What we hear every day, via the media
- What we've been told while growing up

TALK SENSE TO YOURSELF

An achiever is a believer, depending on the degree of self-esteem. If you are an under-achiever, shine the searchlight of awareness into the shadows of your past. Memory makes the difference between success or failure. You can only be as good as memories allow you to think you are.

See past events in perspective. Take an honest, penetrating look at your present-day weaknesses. How did they get a hold on you in the first place? Don't be afraid to face the truth. Relax in the knowledge that the past is largely erasable with hypnotic techniques.

You may not realize it at this moment, but, awake and asleep, you are constantly telling yourself things about yourself, both good and bad. The most forceful persuader we have is our own inner commanding voice. It can be a tyrant or a savior.

What are you telling yourself about yourself unconsciously? Much of our inner thinking is uncomplimentary to ourselves. We have been trained by society to be self-critical. The average person's self-evaluation follows the pattern established by parents and schools who expected everyone to conform to rules that may not suit each individual, unique personality.

Many people cling to a negative image of themselves. In so doing, they confirm and compound their imagined inadequacies. A troublesome thought may be just a fleeting one (even one word) but once apprehension stirs your spinal cord your brain sets up its defeatist reaction.

OPTIMIZING YOUR TALENTS

There is no limit to what your imagination can conjure up to spur your latent abilities and kindle the flame that lights up your goals. Self-talk can make the difference between fulfillment or frustration. Ask yourself: "What am I telling myself about myself? Is it helping me or hindering me?" When you think like a loser, your clever brain digs up all the old defeatist associations to further hamper you. There are also some helpful memories to recall. Everyone has both. Most people have had too many put-downs. The difference between a winner and a loser is that a winner bounces back — higher than before.

Hypnosis puts us in touch with a section of the brain which enables us to become greater than our expectations of self. Honoring your CORE takes you out of the fairy-tale of confused emotions to rational reality. The ability to perform unusual physical feats is an art that anyone is capable of. We can see in the sports arena, where gold medal winners "psyche" themselves up to surpass the records of others as well as their own.

KEEP YOUR EYE ON THE GOAL

Because the average person is unable to concentrate his thoughts along a single line of endeavor, he fails more than he succeeds in many areas of living. Self-sabotaging behavior underlies most stories of "almost made it," or downright failure. Possibility thinking comes with acceptance of positive suggestion. With it comes abundant hope which can eradicate despair and inertia.

The best and most effective way to get speedy results from self-suggestion is to be systematic about it. Setting aside a special study-relaxation time, and being consistent about it is the only way to affect the necessary changes. Getting into the habit of self-help is easier than perpetuating self-defeat.

CHANGE BAD HABITS TO BETTER ONES

The human personality is made up of a collection of reflex habits. All of our activities center around these patterns of automatic habit. In order for you to reach your goals, you must be wide awake to your own entrenched habits and keep asking yourself, "Is this action helping me get where I want to go, or is it hindering me?" Remember that you always have the power to decide between a negative or positive reaction to outside stimulus. Determine what your true desires are, and do not continue a habit if you know it is contrary to your needs.

ENERGIZE YOUR MAGNETIC POWER

After going into hypnosis, see yourself radiating a shining golden aura. Its magnetic energy attracts to you everything and everyone you need to succeed. You see people who can help you. They are drawing closer to you. Now you are surrounded by a team of experts who believe in you. If it's money you need in order to fulfill your dream, see it materialize. You believe in yourself and others follow your lead.

Now you watch yourself, taking all the steps necessary to get where you want to go. See yourself do the following:

- Wake up in the morning raring to go! Full of energy!

- Examining your plan for the day, enthusiastically.

- You receive calls from team members. You call others.

- You are attending a celebration to honor your work.

- You are thanking people who have assisted you.

They praise your achievements. Ask questions of your high image and listen to the practical advice presented to you.

Self-talk: "I will gain great insight from this experience. It will mature me and bring me enlightenment as to how I can improve myself in this lifetime. I will return to this imagery whenever I need greater insight into my future."

BREAK BLOCKS BY EXAMINING THE PAST

If sabotage is self inflicted, there is a way to blast the obstructive block. Enter your hypnotic center to see past events in their proper perspective. Take an honest, penetrating look at your present-day inadequacies. How did they get a hold on you in the first place? Don't be afraid to face the truth. Let your mind freely wander around the worst incidents of your life. Contemplate on how the past may still be influencing you. Self-examination, if it is thorough, is always the first step toward change. No one who enters deep hypnosis remains the same.

SURROUND YOURSELF WITH A TEAM

Influencing others begins with convincing yourself that you are worthy of success. The most gratifying success comes from a passion for excellence, based on your own sensibilities. It always involves self-appreciation.

DON'T EVER GIVE UP YOUR DREAMS

Stick to it; lack of persistence hinders success. Thomas Alva Edison was fired with dogged determination to devise a way to lighten space without candles. He invented the light bulb and influenced all electronic invention which followed. As a school child I visited his workshop in New Jersey where he had lived. My teacher pointed to a cot near his workbench.

There was a small, yellowed sign above the cot, which read: "This is where I dream-up my inventions." The tour guide explained that he conceived his inventions during short naps (we can safely surmise that he entered his CORE with self-hypnosis).

Mr. Edison held nearly 1,100 invention patents, and was in the vanguard of many future inventions in electronics. His creation of the light bulb, phonograph, movie camera and projector, paved the way for hundreds of industries.

CLIMB FURTHER UP THE LADDER

While hypnosis frequently elevates the status of already successful people, it is also invaluable for encouraging those who lack sufficient self-esteem and confidence to get started. It helps you readjust your priorities, especially those that govern your time and the energy previously wasted on non-goal oriented activity which brings no reward.

For success oriented people hypnosis can be a quantum leap to the epitome of their innate capabilities. Once you learn to flip the switch from NO to ON, you will connect your brain to physical action and radiate a glow of success. No one can make you successful but yourself. Your successes and failures both emanate from your own previous programming. YOU are the only one who possesses the proper instrument to correct past mistakes — that very personal instrument is your own mind which constantly directs you. Get into the drivers seat and get to your destination; make the right turn at the crossroads; and take the highway to self-fulfillment.

Because the average person is unable to concentrate his thoughts along a single line of endeavor, he fails more than he succeeds many areas of living. You can achieve your own perfection through inner direction and live your life powerfully — make your own personal miracles. Many people sabotage their own success just as they are on the verge of getting to their goals.

The drive to sink one's own ship takes over and losers do themselves in with a strange perverse urge to avoid the burdens of success. Many otherwise normal people, subconsciously anticipate failure, and by so doing sabotage themselves. One of the tragedies of life is that so many people spend their lives without even knowing that their thoughts are blocking success. Feeling like a loser happens on an unaware level. It develops from behaving like a loser. How do you stop the self-defeating cycle? Start by thinking of the way success will make you feel, and soon you will feel the way you think.

Psychologists tell us that we have mixed associations (subliminal suggestions) linked to both pleasure and pain, if we achieve our desires. We can stop self-sabotage by identifying the defeating thought. Once we do so, we can reconvert reflexes from negative response to positive. You cannot succeed at anything if your mind expects failure.

Many otherwise normal people subconsciously anticipate failure and by so doing, sabotage themselves. One of the tragedies of life is that most people spend their lives never knowing their thoughts are interfering with their degree of success. Once you have the right ATTITUDE, take ACTION, and you will ACHEIVE your desires. With the right attitude, loose pieces begin to fall into place. Optimism opens the gate to realization and floods the mind with anticipation.

IMPROVING PERCEPTION OF SELF

Use your creative imagery to paint a new self-portrait one that does yourself full justice. Pained emotions twist the picture like a reflection in a distorted mirror. Clearing up this mottled reflection takes reconditioning through deep hypnosis with enhanced visualization.

Always perceive yourself in the driver's seat of your life instead of a passenger going on someone else's success trip. Some people are even less aware. They just sit in the back seat and never see where they're going. Take over the journey. Get a road-map — a life's plan. Avoid the pot holes and stay on track. Make the right turn at crossroads and move forward on the high road to meaningful goals. When a person is lost, or thinks like a loser, the brain digs up defeatist associations that set up road-blocks to progress.

Sometimes success requires changing careers to work in a field more compatible with one's talents and desires. Where learning is required to bridge the gap into a new area, the power of mind brings tenacious determination to move onward and upward.

KEEP YOUR MIND OPEN AND EAGER

Respond enthusiastically about new ideas that might be of help to you. Your mind is like a huge tape recorder of unlimited capacity. If you wish to become more positive than negative, you must develop a system to wipe off "the tape" and replace misinformation with proper directions for living. Unless you do this, you will be cheating yourself out of the kind of life that can only come from running your machinery on all its cylinders.

The only worthwhile thing to learn from the past is how to avoid repeating the same mistakes over again. Mistakes are part of life's experiences, and the only person who never makes a mistake is one who never attempts anything. Stewing in old juices of despair only serves to seep them deeper into the flesh of our minds and souls. Decide to make a fresh start.

YOU ARE YOUR OWN MIRACLE WORKER

You can achieve your own perfection through inner direction and live your life powerfully — make your own personal miracles. Many people sabotage their own success just as they are on the verge of getting to their goals. The drive to sink one's own ship takes over and they do themselves in with a strange perverse urge to avoid the pressure of success.

Psychologists tell us that we have mixed word associations (subliminal suggestions) linked to both pleasure and pain if we should achieve the desired results. We can eliminate this self-sabotage by identifying the defeating thought that has become an obstacle. Once we do so, we can use the erasing and replacing technique to switch the reflexes from negative to positive.

No matter how difficult problems seem to be, do not underestimate your powerful influence upon destructive behavior. You can reshape and remold automatic responses by teaching yourself constructive behavior, instead. People not only become adjusted to a way of behaving; they can also become de-adjusted.

Self-realization can only follow the footsteps of self-visualization. To understand the kind of person you are today you need to examine the kind of child you were yesterday. Is that inner child still haunting you? The forces of the past that influence your present attitude and actions must be examined with the wisdom of maturity. Once you look at the past honestly, you can set it aside and not permit it to throttle your machinery.

Like a computer, you can program your mind to properly activate your life and reach wanted goals. However, the output can only be as good as the input. What are you putting into your mind? When you elevate your thinking, your brain automatically functions on a higher level. All the good that can come to you in your lifetime must come through your own thinking.

COMMON HABITS OF LOSERS

Procrastination — Putting off till tomorrow what you should do today, ensures that your success never materializes.

Lack of Planning — Plan your work and work your plan. Organize with a place for everything and everything in its place.

Blaming Others — Take responsibility for getting the job done. No one can block you if you are determined to forge ahead.

AUTO-SUGGESTIONS - LADDER TO SUCCESS

Auto-suggestions are self-commands. If they start the mind and body moving in the right direction, they are the right kind of suggestions. Thought activators bring about affirmative improvements. Remember, all suggestion, past and present, is transformed into auto-suggestion by failure to reject. If you desire to be more than a puppet, you must evaluate each outside suggestion before making it your own.

FINGER-TAP SUCCESS EXPECTATIONS

Tap your forefinger with each repetitive suggestion. This technique brings together the mind and body, while at the same time tapping the thought into the automatic motor system. Silent suggestion can be practiced effectively no matter where we happen to be, without anyone being aware we are doing it.

If you see an important wealthy executive tapping his finger on his desk, he may be a graduate of this method. Constant repetition is important because the more often you suggest success to yourself, the sooner it will happen. Each time you make a success suggestion to your mind, you accumulate the power of this activating force and teach your mind to flash the right messages to you in time of need.

The title of the film is "My Future"... Pick a date for reaching a goal — six months, a year, or ten years. You can change the date each time you practice this unique method. Watch yourself enjoying the improvements that you desire. Imagine an awards celebration. You are being honored for your success. Attractive, intelligent people surround you. They show their respect and admiration. Next, picture yourself in a fabulous home. See yourself depositing checks. Money has been rolling in. You have an excellent relationship. See whatever it is you wish to be. Always remember: Visualize to actualize.

THINK AND SPEAK WITH POWER

Thinking has motivational power in any direction. If your thoughts are of a defeatist nature, you are surely going to be defeated. However, if you think and speak as a winner, you cannot help but act like a winner and overcome adversities. Your wonderous brain is constantly exercising control over both the involuntary and voluntary systems of your body. It determines all of its action based on records and memories of past suggestion. When you think like a loser, your clever brain digs up all the old defeatist associations to further hamper you. There are also some helpful memories to recall if you really wish to do so. Everyone has both. Check and notice your responses.

CORE hypnosis is a proven method of focusing on a wanted condition. It frees the mind to expect improvement when thinking about oneself. This ability to aspire to greater levels of feeling and thinking is the fundamental way in which humans differ from all the other forms of life upon our planet.

SUGGESTION: "I will gain great insight from this experience. It will guide me to improve myself in this lifetime. Each time I choose to go into this dimension, I will gain more and more information to help myself."

Do not let outside thoughts blur the lucidity of the memory that you must study and correct. Examine your past dispassionately, as if you are gazing through a window, darkly, secure in the warm comfort of your home. Think of your past as a replay of an old, obsolete movie. Notice how outdated your emotions are in relationship to your present-day needs.

You are now examining your past with logic and rationality instead of emotional involvement. Here are some tips on making the most of your self-analysis.

— See yourself at your worst.
— Recall the incident in detail.
— Where were you?
— Who was with you?
— What conversation took place?
— What happened to your confidence?

Meditate on other people's motivations. Be flexible and open-minded and also emotionally calm. Once you establish contact with your inner self you will be able to clear away the emotional debris so that you can examine your past realistically. The formula is as easy as ABC and can be applied to any area of personal enrichment. Making the decision to improve by examining and eliminating past problems.

There are always two ways to go. One is the way most people go, around in a circle. The other is a straight line to your goal, which is your own unique, extraordinary version of success.

When past memories in relation to fulfillment are full of stress, the brain causes apprehension. However, when these images are wiped out, tension subsides and so does anxiety. Erasing old images clears the mind, into which you will engrave new, helpful images of success. Taking a limited look backward makes it possible to take unlimited steps forward.

MAKE A COMMITMENT TO YOURSELF

Don't hang on the brink of indecision. Clarify your immediate aim and your eventual goal. For example, your immediate goal might be: Receiving a raise. Your long-term goal — owning your own business

Because it is proven that imagination is more powerful than knowledge, a person's success is strengthened or weakened as a result of what he imagines himself capable of. Imagery is the art of using fantasy to conjure up mind-pictures that serve as a guide in real-life situations. An improved image builds confident expectations that turn the tide from merely wanting to succeed to actually doing so.

The mind's perception of improvement speeds the relearning process, even though the perception is only in the imagination. Your imagination can also erase thoughts of impending failure and fear of inadequacy. You can replace negative fantasies with visions of success. This eludes most people, yet everyone has the innate capacity to accomplish their aims according to their individual potential. Hypnosis helps us discover what that potential is: it digs up old defeatist thought associations and then proceeds to wipe them out.

There are also some helpful memories that you can recall if you really wish to do so. Everyone has both. Check and notice your responses. Enter your hypnotic center; then check out what you have been telling yourself that might be hampering you.

Suggestion: "I will gain great insight from this experience. If success is to be, it is up to me."

No one can make you successful but yourself. Success and failure both emanate from previous programming. YOU are the only one who possesses the proper instrument to correct past mistakes — that very personal instrument is your own mind which constantly directs you. We have been drilled, more or less, to be ashamed of self-praise, yet self appreciation can strengthen motivation, so essential to build a positive, worthy-of-success, self-image.

A SCRIPT FOR SPEEDING UP SUCCESS

Visualization... Strolling along on a beautiful day, you see a movie house with your name on the marquee. You go in and sit down and watch the screen. You are the viewer, the star, the director and producer. The title of the film is "My Goals." Pick a date for reaching a goal,— six months, a year, or ten years. You can change the date each time you practice this unique method. Watch yourself enjoying the improvements that you desire. People admire you. Money rolls in. Possibility thinking comes with acceptance of positive suggestion. With it comes abundant hope which can eradicate despair and inertia.

FLIP THE SUCCESS SWITCH - NO TO ON

You must choose whether you wish to perpetuate outmoded, unsatisfactory attitudes and responses or whether you are ready to embrace life fully. If the latter is true there is nothing to stand in your way but yourself. Every time you think and every time you speak, you should know that each thought and word brings with it a physical action and a possible effect upon your body.

Suggestion has unlimited power in both directions. You can use it to Uplift or

Downgrade your chances to succeed. If your thoughts are of a defeatist nature, you are surely going to be defeated. However, if you think and speak as a winner, you cannot help but act like a winner and win out over adversities. Your wondrous brain is constantly exercising control over both the involuntary and voluntary systems of your body. It determines all of its action based on records and memories of past suggestion. When you think like a loser, your clever brain digs up all the old defeatist associations to further hamper you. There are also some helpful memories to recall if you really wish to do so. Everyone has both. Check and notice your responses. Check and notice what you are telling yourself about yourself.

Always keep your mind open and eager, enthusiastically curious about new ideas that might be of help to you. Your mind is like a huge tape recorder of unlimited capacity. If you wish to become more positive than negative you must develop a system for wiping off "the tape" and replacing misinformation with proper directions for living.

EVERYONE CAN SUCCEED AT SOMETHING

I had an interesting conversation with an artist, who learned to cope with cerebral palsy by painting with his feet. The result was breathtaking artistry. He gives thousands of people pleasure with his beautiful land and seascapes. He is so busy painting and arranging to sell his works of art that he has no time or thought to feel sorry for himself. He is an inspiration to all that have the pleasure of his company. He is proof the disabled can be enabled if they are determined to make the most of their assets. By his accomplishments, he proves that handicaps can be surmounted and life enhanced through altering defeatist attitudes to self-fulfilling activities.

CHAPTER 8

SPIRITUAL AND PSYCHIC DEVELOPMENT

Past-life Regression - Transmigration
You Can Become Your Own Best Psychic

Where do we go after we have corrected the impact of negative programming? This is a time to search for deeper meaning, for answers to the puzzle of life, time to embrace higher values, such as Truth, Beauty, Goodness, and Love. This heightened spiritual insight can be attained, once we are able to enter the CORE (Center of Radiant Energy), and are ready to explore.

The spirit level helps nurture intuitive power to enrich life. Not every practitioner of hypnosis and self-hypnosis can achieve a spiritual "high." However, any level of hypnosis can enable the user to improve in dozens of ways. Some people who start out as light subjects, eventually reach their (CORE) spirit level by consistent practice.

While CORE hypnosis brings results based on centering, the spiritual trance allows feelings to flow without limitations. You enter a space that can only be called, "amorphous." This mystical feeling will be recognized by you as transcending time and space. There is a Chinese poem, by Loa Tzu, that expresses the power of letting go:

"Life's mystery lies in muddy water.
How shall I perceive this mystery?
Water becomes still through stillness.
How then, can I become still?
By flowing with the stream."

WHAT CAN ONE DO IN A SPIRITUAL TRANCE?

Various people, who have mastered the "out-of-body" trance report the following experiences — they say they can: Intensify intuition. Gain Psychic Insight. Establish telepathic communication between self mind and another person, regardless of geographic distance. A nurse client tells me she can shine a light of comfort, for her patients, at time of death. Another person said, "I have become my own fortune-teller, my own psychic healer, and spirit guide to higher consciousness."

You can tap and expand creativity, sensitivity, and insight. These are the qualities that poets, artists, writers, inventors, philosophers, and other creative people have been acutely aware of. Their sensitivities convinced them that spiritual value is of more lasting importance than the material.

Many scientists and world leaders have acknowledged that their most valuable innovative decisions have emerged, without conscious effort, from the subterranean recesses of the mind. These bight jewels of ideas may be unprocessed like a diamond in the rough, which they had to refine and polish to brilliance.

Subconscious inspiration, which takes place before mathematical deductions, is primarily responsible for human progress. It is as if, each of us has a genius within which prompts amazing leaps to higher attainment. The unique characteristics which we each exhibit, are fundamentally derived from a combination of hereditary endowments and our individual life experiences. This accounts for the fact that we are each one, unprecedented and unrepeatable as a person. Because of this factor, spiritual hypnosis takes on a personal quality that is custom-made for one and all.

EMOTIONS CAN MARK THE BODY

Embarrassment makes some people blush or sweat. Others break out in hives. Religious passion can cause stigmata, a reproduction of the wounds Christ received on the cross. Stigmata were believed to be supernaturally induced and led to the Pope bestowing the honor of Sainthood upon the stigmatized. Not all such cases have been authenticated. A distinction is made by the church between scars caused by visualization alone and those spiritually imposed.

Theologians do not ignore the possibility that power of the mind may have been involved. Those of us who work in holistic methods to help cure psychosomatic illness know the brain's connection to physical responses. We know that whenever a suggestion is repeated over and over again, it becomes a conditioned reflex.

The power of suggestion, coupled with faith, explains many religious and metaphysical "miracles." For example, in Haiti, when Voodoo participants are in a trance they are able to walk on fire and glass, to pierce their skin without bleeding.

THE POWER IS WITHIN EACH OF US

To those who devote their lives to spiritual value, this immediate life is simply the threshold, the waiting room. Life may be difficult and suffering acute, but only a transition to a better place where there is freedom from earthly problems.

Realists take a pragmatic point of view and believe that both material and spiritual can exist in harmony and bring greater health and happiness for everyone. We are all capable of using our sixth sense — Extra Sensory Perception. It is an extension of our intelligence, a natural innate power, but rarely liberated in most people.

Deep CORE hypnosis is necessary to bypass critical resistance, due to fear of the unknown dimension of mind. Spirituality is enhanced in the deep hypnotic CORE, bringing reverence for life, vigor to the weak, and clarity to the confused. You can awaken the ecstatic self and move forward on a joyous path to encounter your spiritual self.

Any negative effects of childhood, such as abuse or trauma, can be understood and erased. This will awaken compassion in your heart to forgive those that did not understand what they were doing. It will guide you to magnetize all that is good, affirming life and spiritual exaltation. Here are a few basic affirmations:

"I feel uplifted, and will never be downgraded again."
"I am letting my parents go and healing my wounded child."
"I am safe, calm, at peace. I accept myself completely."
"I have everything I need to enjoy every moment of life."
"Every day, in every way, I am happier and healthier."

You can create your own phrases, according to your individual needs. Notice that all affirmation are in the present tense, because it helps to speed positive changes if you think that improvement has already taken place.

THE PLACE WHERE HUNCHES ARE BORN

Hunches come with a burst of intuition from the deepest crevices of the subconscious. When it happens, which may be at inopportune moments, we can either forgo it — or go for it! Hunches have a paradoxical quality that is both inner created and yet seems to descend as an offering, or blessing from the unknown. This perception expands the boundaries of the mind as one realizes the twin sense of being detached and separated from the thought, while simultaneously, in full control. Hunches are both mystical and real. Following through requires courage and an element of risk-taking. To decide if the risk is worth the reward, one has to contemplate the wisest action to take.

In an awake, conscious state, we usually ignore hunches because they become confused with everyday thinking, lost like a needle in a haystack. We all experience strong feelings to do or not to do something, yet most of us bypass the urge, because there is no provable explanation as to why this happens.

Later, if something happens to verify your hunch, you may not remember or recognize it's importance. Most people explain their hunches as coincidence or happenstance. It's different when you are focused in profound hypnosis. Something special happens when you get a hunch while in a spiritual trance; that kind of hunch has power because you know that it is a message, coming from a higher source.

When you are centered in your intuitive mind, physicality is set aside and every thought becomes a voyage of discovery. As you relinquish critical judgment, you find yourself flowing into a soft, misty whirlpool, into the receptive center of your subconscious. Here, time stands still. In this space of total calmness, you can communicate with your spiritual self.

This is a time when we cease to live unreflectively, a time to affirm life with reverence, and lift our spirits high. Not only does the spirit soar, but this is also the moment when spontaneous, therapeutic healing takes place. Once you are firmly centered, the force of liberation from pain and illness is directed into the malady by visualizing personal perfection in that area of body or mind.

CAN WE PROVE EXTRA SENSORY PERCEPTION?

Not yet. However, there are theories. We do know that with all ESP phenomena, faith and confidence encourage the process, while fear and doubt do the opposite. One theory is that the brain emits energy from its electromagnetic field in the form of vibrations. Scientific investigation tells us that brain electricity can be measured and recorded on an electroencephalograph.

Perhaps, some day there will be a scientific method to record Extra Sensory Perception. Until then, here are some thoughts that I have heard expressed at gatherings of psychologists, as well as practitioners in the metaphysical field. We know that television and radio waves are vibrated through space. It might occur to one that the mind functions in a similar way as a radio.

In radio or in using a phone, when a certain station or person is wanted, the dial is set or the number tapped as the sender is tuned in to the receiver. All this happens through transmission of wave lengths, or vibrations in the currents of air, which surround us. Rhythmic vibrations are accepted as a necessary part of life, which is in constant motion. As the earth moves, it stirs the atmosphere surrounding it, and causes constant changes in the magnetic attraction of objects.

Have you noticed that when people meet there is an instant sense of acceptance, or rejection on a subliminal level. We are constantly sending each other 'vibes,' which can alter our interaction in a negative, or positive way. It's part of nature. As the rolling sea breaks its ripples onto the shore, it changes the look of the sand. All images constantly vary, so do our eyes through which we view them. Vibrations birth the morning that drifts into noon, then sunset and darkness.

The cycle repeats itself endlessly. Every tree, every blade of grass has its own individual replay. The breeze rustles the trees and sways its branches, which sets each leaf into new vibrations of its own. Our rhythmic vibrations play an important part in our relationships. This is the basis for being attracted to some people and repulsed by others.

TELEPATHY—COMMUNICATING THOUGHTS

People are, in a way, like leaves, stirred by the rhythm of those that surround them. Telepathy is the power of the mind to project thoughts to another person — without any electronic device. Transference of thought between two people, while they are in an altered state is extremely impressive. A time is agreed upon and each person goes into the spiritual trance level. They can be in the same room or separated in different cities or countries far beyond the sea. Distance is not the decisive factor. Telepathy extends far beyond the place or moment it is perceived.

A telepathic experience was described to me this way: "I followed the induction and visualization techniques which you taught me in your seminar, with these results. I fixed my mind on Michael's forehead until I could see his face, distinctly. At that point I projected a light to the center of his forehead and pictured it penetrating into the center of his brain.

"After sustaining that focus for a few seconds, I suddenly got a rush of feeling that I had made mental contact with him. It's the kind of sensation you have to feel yourself to understand the thrill that ripples through your nerves. I received from him the receptivity that you get when you insert a plug a into a socket and a light goes on. There is a feeling of having actual nearness to the person, not just body closeness, but also, the sensitized exchange of spiritual energy.

"I saw flashes of events surrounding him. I saw he was in danger of a car accident. This prompted me to call him on the phone. I was not surprised when he told me that he had been rear-ended in traffic and was relieved when he assured me he had escaped with minor injuries."

CHANNELING TO A PERSON WHO IS DECEASED

There are some individuals, who are especially skilled in the art of extra sensory communication. Many are trained in the art of self-hypnosis. These mediums, frequently seen on television interviews, claim that they can contact people who have lived previously. This appears to be of great solace and comfort to those who wish to reach them. The gift of clairvoyance may be discovered, accidentally while a person is in a deep trance, or during sleep, while dreaming.

HYPNOSIS FOR METAPHYSICAL TRAINING

This is unique, extremely effective way to help metaphysical practitioners expand their talents. Many mediums have asked for hypnotic training to sharpen their skills. In an ultra-depth healing trance our spirit awakens, and the soul reveals what the mind conceals. We feel the beauty of life and thrill to the secret of love. Referred in metaphysical literature as the "third (inner) eye," the trance provides:

A place to confront the shadows of your past;
A time to contemplate the nature of the soul;
A way to examine one's future, psychic destiny;
An opportunity to talk with Guardian Angels;
A method to gain insight to parapsychology;
A place to fire up your secret inner healer;
A searchlight to illuminate roots of problems;
A path to guide you toward out-of-body travel;
A method permitting you to do automatic writing.

IN ADDITION YOU CAN:

Intensify intuition and learn to channel;
Develop clairvoyance, become your own psychic;
Project a radiant aura to magnetize success;
Become a spiritual guide to enhance others.

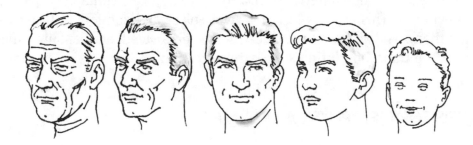

EXPLORE PAST-LIFE FOR GUIDANCE

You can request your intuitive mind to advise you in making the right decisions when you find yourself at a cross-road. You can also ask to be warned if there are obstacles or pitfallls to be wary of. Spiritual, deep CORE hypnosis often results in metaphysical enlightenment. It shines light on a pathway to find hidden truths and better understanding for mastering life's challenges.

We can also confer with a wise person whom we may or may not have encountered to act as a spirit guide to bring wisdom in situations that are beyond our limitations. For example an inventor might ask questions of a creative genius like Edison.

Looking into a past life cannot change what happened in the past, but we can change who we have become because of what happened. At a spiritual trance level, we free ourselves from past trauma and create a better future by reviewing and learning. This is the method to demystify the unknown, observe your past, dispassionately with profound insight. This provides the information to a better future. You can make time-lines work for you by understanding the times that have past.

THREE TYPES OF REGRESSION:

1. To Recall Some Specific Incident
2. To Investigate Childhood trauma
3. To Uncover Secrets Of Past Lives

VISUALIZATION - See yourself standing in front of a blackboard. Visualize a large white circle on the blackboard. See yourself in the center of the circle. Now the circle turns into a long tunnel with a light shining in the distance. You find yourself on a moving sidewalk, passing through the length of the tunnel, headed toward the golden light that is very beautiful. When you reach the light you will be in another lifetime. Notice a calendar indicating the year.

See the color of your skin. Are you a man or a woman, adult or child? What do the other people call you? What part of the world is this? Listen to the language being spoken. Attend a ritual ceremony. Taste the food. Smell the aromas. Listen to the music. Ask questions. Tell yourself: "I will gain great insight from this experience. It will mature me and bring me enlightenment to improve myself in this lifetime. Each time I choose to go into this dimension, I will gain more and more information to help myself."

HOW TO DEEPEN TRANCE-MEDITATION

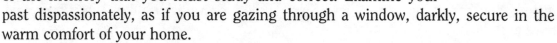

If outside thoughts crowd into the stream of your ideation, don't give them a harbor. Just let them pass in and out of your consciousness, for they are negative resistance to positive change. Do not let outside thoughts infiltrate or they will blur the lucidity of the memory that you must study and correct. Examine your past dispassionately, as if you are gazing through a window, darkly, secure in the warm comfort of your home.

Be the observer, the audience. Think of your past as a replay of an old, obsolete movie. Notice how outdated your emotions are in relationship to your present-day problems. You are now examining your past with logic and rationality instead of emotional involvement. Look for meaning beyond the present limitations of time and space. Feel a sense of immortality, as you link mind and body to spirit.

THE FASCINATION OF REINCARNATION

Although there is no scientific proof of reincarnation, there are aspects that seem recognizable and assessable. Even though we are at present incapable of weighing and measuring the phenomenon, we cannot discount a theory accepted by two-thirds of the world's population. Eastern religions believe memories from previous lives are retained in primitive brain crevices, influencing behavior in the present life. Since the beginning of human history, peoples have shared the belief that the human soul is indestructible. Whether one accepts the concept of soul, spirit or super-brain, the belief follows and we are more than matter and our bodies are only the visible evidence of being. Belief in reincarnation opens endless possibilities for past life influences. It is worthy of scientific investigation.

TRANSCENDENCE - TURN OFF AND TUNE IN

Whereas most hypnosis is concerned with mind and matter, where there is a subject with an objective as a goal, spiritual ascendance is non-demanding and open to allow the unexpected. Instead of zeroing into a specific spot, there is an acceptance of a higher power directing the pathway. Transcendence opens new channels to intuitive experience.

Transcendental hypnosis can serve as the threshold to deep nighttime sleep and set the stage for dreaming dreams of significance. You can train yourself to interpret a dream for its guidance value. In addition, if you wish, you can direct a dream, about a subject you want to understand better. Research suggests that we can gain control over our dreams. Some people have developed the ability to monitor their dreams as if they are onlookers at a movie screening. This has proven a valuable method to gain submerged information from the subconscious mind.

Lucid dreaming can be called creative dreaming because new inventive ideas present themselves in images. Several artists and writers whom I have trained, are able to work out details of their creation in a dream-like state. In some cases they are able to make notes while remaining in a trance state.

SOUL - MATING THROUGH SEXUAL BONDING

There is a chemistry that exists between people that either attracts or repels. Soul-mating does not usually happen at first meeting. It takes time for the emotional and mental interaction to intertwine. It takes a kind of emotional, rhythmic process of exchanging pieces of the mysterious puzzle of life. When we reach spiritual contemplation, we send out rhythms to attract someone on the same high plane of awareness. This is accomplished by opening the sensory gateways that link one to the other. It is through the functioning of our senses that we eliminate separation of thought. Because there has been so much blocking off and diversion of feeling, we must now deliberately teach ourselves that there is more to life's fulfillment than the physical.

Spiritual ascendance begins by first freeing your five senses from the five little cubbyholes of your conscious mind, so that they can lead you to your "sixth sense." Only when all six senses are interwoven, can you bring about spiritual bonding, the kind of unified togetherness that bridges the gap between body and soul. When reciprocal bonding is missing, so is total fulfillment. This is what makes humans unique among all other species.

NEW LOVERS MAY NOT BE STRANGERS

"It seems that we have met before," is echoed in poetry and song around the world. One poet wrote, "Oh strange, that in our embers there is something that remembers!" The "deja vu" phenomenon may be part of the belief that each life is a recurring one, linked to cyclical vibrations. This in a universal process where everything in nature is ruled by the law of renewal. Since the beginning of human history, peoples have shared the belief that the human soul is indestructible. If one accepts the concept of soul, the belief follows that we are more than just physical matter, more than the visible evidence of life and permanent death.

TRANSMIGRATION — SOUL TRAVEL

Followers of Eastern religions accept transmigration without question. Ancient Egyptians embalmed the bodies of their dead to preserve them for reincarnation. The early Greek philosopher, Pythagoras, assured the citizenry that the soul, being only temporarily confined to its earthly body, survived after death.

After a series of rebirths in changing bodies, the soul was to be released from its cycle of reincarnation, and able to ascend to a permanent place in the spiritual hemisphere. Eastern religions believe memories from previous lives are retained in primitive brain crevices, influencing behavior in the present life.

There are additional bonuses, such as an increase in awareness, discovery of your life's purpose. Also, making peace with that which is inevitable, like aging and death. While in a spiritual trance, you can also develop the gift of healing, yourself--and others. Above all, feeling vibrant joy in living in the moment, knowing the answers to: Who Am I? Why am I here? Where am I going? How can I get there? If you don't have the answers to those life-enhancing questions, go into spiritual hypnosis and the answers will present themselves.

VISUALIZE YOUR SPIRITUAL CENTER

In using psychic prophecy for self-improvement, you are harnessing right-brain imagery and putting it to work. It becomes a control method of predicting how you will behave at a given time, because you are making use of the human gift of imagination, which we are privileged to possess.

Here is a visualization that will enhance your hypnosis meditation: "You are strolling along on a beautiful day, walking through a garden. Your senses are keenly responsive. You see the colors of the flower. Smell their aroma. Feel a summer breeze caress your skin. Listen and remember serene, spiritual music. Recall the taste of ripened fruit. You are walking on a path leading to a golden temple at the top of a green, grassy hillside. The door is wide open. You see a welcome mat with your name on it. You go in and see a radiant light cascading down through the crystal dome of the temple.

Stand in the radiant golden light. You are surrounded on all sides. Let it seep into the top of your head. Now a halo of light surrounds your forehead, and as you absorb the blessing, it flows and glows down over your face and neck...into your arms and through your chest...into your heart. Now you are encased in a bubble of golden light... You are now inner directed, and spiritually protected. As you walk from the temple. You find yourself on the top of the hill. Picture a spiritual vision of yourself reaching your arms up toward the heavens and feeling exalted. Feel peaceful and notice a renewal of healthy energy. You are at one with the universe.

REBIRTHING TECHNIQUE TO DETOX

After completing the above imagery, take yourself even deeper to clarify and cleanse past pain and trauma. You are at the top of the hillside looking down into a fertile valley. See the swaying treetops and see a serene lake nestled between the trees. Feel the breeze caressing your skin as you drift down into the valley. A sense of weightlessness takes over. All gravity has vanished, both gravity of the earth's surface and gravity of emotions. You are free now. You are floating down. Down, down.

I will count down from 10 to 0, and when I reach zero you will find yourself descending into the blissful valley. Now you are being moved toward the lake by a gentle breeze. The lake is a place where you can rebirth yourself. Here you will wash away pain, stress, and anxiety. Rebirthing, also helps to eliminate blocks to success. It will give you the energy to start all over without troublesome baggage from the past.

Stand at the edge of the lake, and contemplate your reflection. See yourself with all the improvements. Reshape your body. See yourself as a winner. Shoulders back head held high. Notice that the water is shallow, safe and clean as you move slowly into its soothing caressing warmth, imagine yourself as a large sponge. Sponge in all that is good and sponge out tension, toxins and trauma. Place mindfulness into the muscles and nerves of your body and let them float aimlessly.

At this point, you are free from your body's demands. Three live-giving forces have combined to nurture you. At this moment you are a spiritual fetus in the womb of the earth. Feel yourself absorbing the three forces of life:

... The divine light which is shining an aura around you and reflects into the water.

... The water that is flowing in and out of every cell, every pore and every organ of your body.

... The oxygen which you are inhaling and reinforcing the life that is growing.

These are the natural forces, without which life could not exist on this planet — light, water, and oxygen. At this time-line you are being purified and made new again. The free-radicals of aging diminish and dissolve. New cells begin to multiply. You are balanced and your aura is sparkling with magnetic radiance. You are experiencing your NOW joyfully and time stands still as the metamorphosis of rebirth takes place. Tell Yourself:

"I am reborn with solutions for a fulfilled life."
"I will return to this warm place for loving guidance."
"Every day, in every way, I am healthier and joyful."

AUTOMATIC WRITING FROM THE SUBCONSCIOUS

There are times when information from the past is needed but the conscious mind does not remember or has blocked the memory because it dredges up emotional pain. If your behavior is not in keeping with your highest ideals and you wonder why you cling to actions or feelings that you should be discarding.

While in a focused trance, you will be able to ask questions of the reluctant mind and receive meaningful answers which will pinpoint solutions. There are two methods which work equally well, depending on individual preference. I suggest you try them both and discover which works best for you.

1. **The Blackboard Technique** - While in trance, do this visualization: Picture yourself standing at a blackboard with chalk in one hand and an eraser in the other. With your chalk, write a short question, such as:

   "Shall I keep my job or quit and get another one?"

   "What can I do to attract a loving soul-mate?"

Write one question at a time. Then erase the question and stare at the empty blackboard. You will see an answer to your question. Your higher mind knows better than anyone else. Record that answer to remember it later.

2. Pad and Pencil Technique - Before you enter hypnosis, prepare a large writing pad and pen within easy reach of your hands. When you reach trance level, picture a clear blue sky with a sky-writing plane waiting for instructions from you. Send a mental question and watch it appear.

Don't force or strain your mind, to articulate clearly. Instead, let it wander. When you see the questions, reach for your pad and pen and, while your eyes are still closed, the thought will flow into your hand and which will write your response to the question.

For both of the above techniques you can use sentence completion, such as follows:

"I have a feeling that......................"
"What I need to say is....................."
"Next time it happens....................."

3. Open Your Eyes Technique - You can also do automatic writing by using Sigmund Freud's word association method. Prepare a list of trigger words like: Mother, Father, Money, Love, etc. When you are still in trance reach for the list and open your eyes and remain focus on the list. Now you will write freely about your emotions associated with the word which you would like to explore.

CLAIRVOYANCE - SEEING WITH EYES CLOSED

This is the ability to see, through extra sensory perception, objects and events distant in time and space. This power is often debated but never totally discredited. In many cases of police investigation, clairvoyants and mediums have come up with information that has assisted crime investigation. This help has centered on finding the locations of bodies that have stumped the police force.

The ability is strengthened by trance induction, in which the medium describes what he/she sees or foresees. Three explanatory theories exist among those who believe in clairvoyance:

1. **That the person is a sensitive vessel, whose organs and voice are entered by some departed spirit entity.**

2. **That the clairvoyant is independent of outside direction and can see people and events beyond normal vision.**

3. **The third point of view is explained as telepathic communication, not with a departed spirit, but between two living minds.**

All agree that some sensitive people can rise above the surface of the conscious mind and transcends reality to acquire telepathic ability.

GLOSSARY

ADVANCED HYPNOSIS ENCYCLOPEDIA FROM A TO Z

IMAGERY AND SUGGESTIONS

* TO THE PROFESSIONAL:
Images and suggestion can be altered to suit individual needs. If a medical problem exists, check with client's physician.

ABERATIONS...
Abnormal compulsions such as sexual fetishes, and fixations may stem from childhood trauma; some cases hark back to parental abuse. The scene can be revisited with hypnotic visualization, automatic writing and counter-suggestion.

Imagery
Use age regression to recall the original source of the fixation. Visualize the beginning of the unwanted behavior. Picture the incident on a screen, and then see a rain storm or a waterfall wash it away.

Suggestion
"The problem is gone and will not return. I will behave normally in every way, from now on. This is permanent correction."

ABILITY/APTITUDE...
If you do not feel fulfilled in what you are doing, use hypnosis to uncover and discover your hidden talents to elevate and enhance your lifestyle. Your subconscious may reveal what your conscious mind tends to conceal. You will understand that your ability and aptitude require self-directed action to be meaningful.

Imagery
Visualize yourself as having fulfilled your desires. Use the "futuristic screen" to see the results you want. Picture a calendar on the wall showing the projected date you plan to reach your goal.

Suggestion
"I have the ability I need to succeed. I am capable. I am organized. I know what I want and how to get it. No one and nothing will block my motivation."

ABORTION...
Women who are deep subjects have reported that they are able to bring about their own abortions in the first trimester, by using self-hypnosis. Self-directed techniques are also used to lower stress during medical abortions, as well as cases where natural miscarriage takes place.

Imagery
After subject reaches trance depth, she is instructed to place her hand on her lower torso just above pubic area and to forcefully exhale, while visualizing the air passing through and out of her vaginal canal. She is told to imagine a deep pink fluid excreted by her uterus, affirming in this way, that there is no pregnancy, and her menstrual period has returned.

Suggestion
"My menstrual period has returned, in a normal way. I'm not pregnant. I am happy and free of worry. When and if, I decide to become pregnant at a later date, I will enjoy a normal pregnancy."

ABUSIVENESS...
Acting out angry impulses can be diminished by practicing mind-control over the automatic reflexes. We respect ourselves to the degree that we are in control of our actions. When we are out of control, we become victims of outside pressures, people or substances.

Imagery
Picture yourself in a challenging situation - the kind that, in the past, caused

you to respond impulsively. Instead of reacting emotionally, stop to think, take five breaths and reconsider your actions. Then change to a more appropriate response.

Suggestion

"I am in control of my behavior. I an taking full responsibility for my actions. I am changing for the better, in every way. I respect the rights of others, and listen to their point of view."

ACCENT...

Whether foreign or regional, hypnosis can retrain your vocal cords, as well as aural perception of sound variations. A rapid method to eliminate accents is to speak into a tape recorder and then listen back when you are under hypnosis. Your mind will be keener. You will notice where you need work.

Imagery

After you reach maximum depth, mental focus is established through localizing your exhalation. As you exhale, visualize a stream of air coming out at the base of your throat, carrying out the accent as you expel the stream of air. Then, while you are inhaling, think of the correct pronunciation.

Suggestion

"I will concentrate on the sound of my voice each time that I speak. I will take time to think before I converse with others. My accent is now gone."

ACCIDENT PRONE...

Consider the law of cause and effect, which says: Every happening has a cause. We have the ability to eliminate the cause and change accidental mishaps. Lack of alertness and perhaps a deep-seated desire to be punishment for believed guilt or wrong-doing, may underlie the carelessness which is part of this problem. It isn't the car that causes the accident, it's the people involved.

Imagery

Recall a past accident and see how it could have been prevented with greater awareness. See yourself at the wheel driving along at a safe speed. You are now concentrating, not only on your own driving, but also on the drivers around you. Then, affirm your mind-control power by the following suggestions:

Suggestion

"I am alert and aware of the seriousness of driving. I will never be a victim nor will I endanger the lives of others." At all times, I will avoid risk."

ACNE CONTROL...

This troubling condition is associated with the over-activity of the sebaceous glands. One factor we can correct is that aggravation increases emotional stress. This why hypnosis has been useful in minimizing the outbreaks in those people who learn self-hypnotic meditation.

Imagery

Before falling asleep, imagine that at you are looking into a mirror, upon awakening in the morning. You are amazed and delighted to find that your skin has cleared up completely.

Suggestion

"I am happy. I am calm. Every day my skin looks better and better. Soon all old signs of skin problems will be gone permanently."

ACCUPUNCTURE...

Nu-Age practitioners are combining their expertise with mental imagery and hypnotic suggestion increasing the effectiveness. Before the needles are put into place, the subject is induced into a light or medium trance

Imagery

The acupuncturist then instructs the subject to imagine a beam of light-energy focused into the area.

Suggestion

The practitioner says: "As I insert the needle, see yourself smiling. Visually anticipate great results. Assure yourself that this procedure will alleviate pain and correct your problem. Next, misdirect your attention to an area of your body far from the spot being worked on."

ADDICTIVE BEHAVIOR...

Addictive behavior is linked to the flux of emotions which constantly surge through the brain. Hypnosis helps us to decide how to respond to emotions, whether to act on weakness or addictive, inappropriate urges, or use restraint. Changing behavior is based on the concept of self-awareness.

Imagery

See yourself surrounded by a group of severely addicted people, who have lost all control of their behavior. Separate yourself from the group and se yourself standing in front of a mirror which is divided in two sections. On one side you see yourself at your worst on the other side of the mirror, picture yourself as a strong individual who has kicked the bad habits.

Suggestion

"I have pride in my character. I can say, NO! and
choose healthier habits that will enrich my life and give me great pride and self-respect."

ADOLESCENCE...

Growth from puberty to maturity has rough spots. The pathway can be made smoother by using self-hypnosis to increase self-esteem and confidence. The young person is given a card upon which to write three wishes that he/she wants to materialize. The hypnotist then directs the visualization.

Imagery

You are on a hilltop, facing another high peak. There is a bridge you can cross that will take you to the other side where you will gain maturity and freedom from anxiety. Holding the rail for security, cross over the bridge, one step at a time. When you bridge the gap, you are welcomed by a group of friends and family members. Now, see yourself at a social gathering, where your wishes are fulfilled.

Suggestion

"I can do anything I put my mind to. I have courage confidence, and motivation to overcome any obstacles."

AEROPHOBIA...

An abnormal fear of wind, gusts of air, drafts and gaseous fumes. These inbred fears will always try to rear their ugly heads and must be slapped down with vigor. Only the zealous and determined ever succeed in changing for the better.

Imagery

Write the problem on a blackboard. See yourself wash it away under a faucet in the sink. Next, see yourself in what once was a threatening situation, facing it casually, with courage and steadfastness. You are aware this is a delusional problem that you have conquered with self applied brain-washing.

Suggestion

"My thinking is no longer cluttered with anxiety and fears. I enjoy everything about nature, including the breeze, that clears the air and clears my mind."

AGE RETARDATION...

Negative expectations tend to affect the degree of body deterioration. Hypnosis can increase longevity by eliminating harmful habits. Humans seldom live a full life span. We could live beyond one hundred years, if we took proper care of ourselves.

Imagery

At medium trance level, go into age regression. See yourself in a three-way mirror, front view, side view, and back view. From every angle, you look younger. Notice a calendar on the wall, flip back the pages to a time when you looked your best. Smile to yourself.

Suggestion

"Every day, in every way, I grow younger. I look younger. I feel younger and healthier. I exercise and eat right. My activities and attitude are young."

AGITOPHASIA...

The person is perceived as being overwrought with anxiety, with little, or no, conscious control of the sound of his/her voice. Breathing is staccato and strained. This condition requires the assistance of a trained therapist who trains the subject to relax, and regulate the voice with rhythm of breathing. It is helpful to record a tape for the client to listen to.

Imagery

After trance induction, deep breathing is directed to the throat and chest areas. Subject visualizes an opening at the solar plexus, showing an "Exit" sign. Focusing strong exhalations, the problem is reduced with repeated positive autosuggestions.

Suggestion

"Each time I speak I sound clearer and clearer. My breathing rhythm is steady and well paced. There's no rush, plenty of time to pause, take a deep breath and gather my thoughts, before I speak."

AGORAPHOBIA...

Anxiety about leaving home and going to strange places, can accelerate to the point of panic attacks (sweating and breathing spasmodically).

Imagery

Phobias require deep hypnosis to be completely obliterated from the sub-conscious. Rehearsing through the "Movie-TV Technique" is effective, when practiced frequently before attempting to act out the problem

Suggestion

"I enjoy seeing new places and new faces. I am normal in every way and look forward to getting out daily."

AIDS (ACQUIRED IMMUNE DEFICIENCY SYNDROME)...

Although caused by a virus, hypnosis can minimize discomfort and symptoms. Anxiety can be lessened by using ultra-depth techniques. Remember, getting into CORE, or spiritual hypnosis, requires practice. With early detection, the trance state can reduce the "viral load," the amount of virus in the blood. Hypnosis is most helpful when combined with medical treatments.

Imagery

Regression is used to a time and place, before the disease took hold. Go back year by year, flipping pages on a giant calendar, until you connect with a healthy period before you had the problem.

Suggestion

"I am improving day by day in every way. My blood count is reaching toward normal. I expect health, and look forward to it and will show definite results."

ALCOHOL...

One third of people in hospital beds are there because of alcohol. The stumbling road of alcohol leads to a dead end and a dead-head. The result is to dull rational thinking. In time the alcoholic becomes lost in a world of alienation, and eventually, self-annihilation. Here's a thought: "First the person takes a drink, then the drink takes a drink, then the drink takes the person."

Imagery

See the split screen. On the negative side, see yourself as you could become — at your worst. On the positive side, see yourself as a sober, successful person. See the alcoholic shrinking as the sober, positive self takes over the entire screen.

Suggestion

"I will stop the habit before the habit stops me. Other people have stayed sober, and so can I. I will live my life one day at a time, and make each day better and better."

ANXIETY ATTACKS...

Events in early life predispose some people to unconsciously re-invent the original trauma. This is correctable with positive reprogramming while under the medium to deep trance state. This enables one to gain clarity about oneself and separate facts from unrealistic worries.

Imagery

This problem calls for regression to early childhood, Using the movie screen helps separate the subject from the immediacy of emotions. Ask for a signal, such as the lifting of a finger when the subject reaches some important event that contributed to the present day anxiety. Provide a pad and pen for writing answers to questions from the hypnotist. You can also use word association here for response.

Suggestion
"I realize the reason for my anxiety and I am ready to change for the better. The past is past. I live in the present moment, without fear."

ALGOPHOBIA...

An unreasonable fear of pain. Not only can the fear be removed, but the pain can actually be diminished and, in cases of motivated subjects, completely erased. A medium trance state is best for this problem because contact needs to be retained in order to focus the mind into a specific area.

Imagery
Select a part of the body which concerns you the most. Place an imaginary magnifying glass over it. Study the shape of the part. Look at the edges of the pain. Visualize a shrinking effect around the spot until it disappears, altogether. See perfection.

Suggestion
Suggestion is best given before the hypnotic state because some subjects go so deep they do not connect with the spoken word. After the subject has been trained, the following suggestion will reinforce the original session: "My pain was subjective and emotional. I have overcome the fear and the pain."

ALLERGIES...

Hypnosis can erase symptoms and even eliminate the problem, for some. If an allergic reaction is seasonal, self hypnosis can be used regularly to postpone and eradicate the occurrence. In addition, you can minimize negative reactions and experience relief without risking side-effects.

Imagery
While under a meditative state of light hypnosis, focused breathing is directed to the respiratory area. Clearing the tubes of the breathing complex is concentrated on. Imagine that the oxygen is coming in and out of the solar plexus.

Suggestion

"I am a sponge. With every breath, I inhale clarity and resistance to allergies. I will not be bothered by sensitive eyes, watery nose, sneezing, or rashes." (Select or add whatever applies to your condition).

AMBIVOLENCE...

The co-existence of antithetical desires, emotions, ideas or goals causes inner friction, indecision, procrastination, and can even cause eventual emotional breakdown. Sort out your real needs and the direction you must take for fulfillment. Remember: "The shortest distance between two points is a straight line."

Imagery

See the blackboard. You have a chalk in one hand, an eraser in the other. Write down your immediate aim and your eventual goal. For example, your immediate aims might be: Increase income. Your ultimate goal: Buy a car, house, etc.

Suggestion

"I will not waste my time going around in circles. I know where I'm going, and I know how to get there."

ANALYSIS...

Psychiatrists may use hypnosis to investigate a patient's mental/emotional history. It always helps to know where we've been in order to figure out where we are going and how to get there.

Imagery

The movie screen technique is very effective in this situation. Depending on when the trauma first took place, the time of regression is generally agreed upon, and then reverse images take the person back in time to review and understand the motivation of those involved. Then, the waterfall visualization is used to wash away the pain and cleanse the psyche for renewal.

Suggestion

"Everything that happened to me in the past was a learning experience from which I have grown into a better person. The past is past. The future starts right now".

ANESTHESIA...

To accomplish this successfully, the subject must enter deep CORE hypnosis. This method lowers the threshold of pain, and is used in some cases for surgery, especially when the patient cannot tolerate drug anesthesia. This is also useful for injections, preparation for operation and dental work.

Imagery

Because pain is conceived in the brain, imagery misdirects the mind's attention to an area away from the pain. This can lesson or completely ameliorate the feeling. Breathing with focus of exhalation directed toward the feet, is very effective, unless the feet are involved. If pain is in the lower extremities, then concentrate on the top of the head for misdirection.

Suggestion

"The pain is gone and will not return. I command my brain — stop the pain!"

ANGER ALEVIATION...

Beneath simmering temper is the anxiety and fear of being hurt. Humiliation tends to trigger a flare up of explosive emotion. Anger makes us more susceptible to disease, from the common cold to serious problems of the immune system.

Imagery

Picture yourself sitting at a table facing the person you are upset with. You are now an arbitrator, rather than an enemy. Make a list of the differences and discuss each one with your opponent. Be flexible and open-minded about the rights of the other person. Listen if you wish to be heard.

Suggestion

"I am ready and willing to compromise and look at both sides of the conflict. I will exercise control and be flexible. If I feel my temper rising, I will count to ten and cool down. I am respected by family and friends for having the character to see both sides."

ANOREXIA...

An alarming epidemic of eating disturbance affects young girls. One out of three teenagers is anorexic or bulimic. Some are only ten years old and weigh less than eighty pounds. A preoccupation with being skinny, based on TV shows, featuring young women with caved-in stomachs and protruding bones. Although Anorexia Nervosa is mostly an affliction of young women, there are also some cases of young men. The disorder has a mortality rate of twenty percent. Eventually, the anorexic may try to gain weight but her body resists. Fortunately, mind and body can become normal with hypnosis.

Imagery

See yourself at the table enjoying your favorite food, a look of contentment and happiness comes over you. Next, you are standing in front of a mirror admiring your new reflection at the proper, healthy weight. You look normal. Attractive. Say to yourself:

Suggestion

"Eating properly is a pleasure. The sight and smell of food stimulates my appetite. At every meal the taste buds become more sensitive as appetite increases to normal. I will only gain up to the normal amount for my age and height and will never become too fat."

APHRODISIAC...

Stronger than man-made concoctions is the sexual power of the mind to stir up a lazy libido, and put the sizzle back in a sexual relationship. As the Buddhists say: "What you think upon grows." It works for both male and female passion.

Imagery

To optimize sexual function and pleasurable feeling, it helps to fantasize. Picture yourself in a sexual embrace, where your libido is steaming hot. See it. Feel it...and make it even better next time.

Suggestion

"Every time I have sex it is more satisfying for myself and partner. I increase sensitive feeling. Because anticipation makes sex better, the next time I expect to have sex, I will think passionate thoughts, and my mind will act like an aphrodisiac."

APPEARANCE...

You can only look as good as your internal vision of yourself. Your right brain is the artist that paints the portrait for your left brain to actualize. This is a time to enhance visualization.

Imagery

See yourself as perfect as you can be. Use the mirror technique. Imagine a split screen; one half is the worst appearance, the other side shows the best. Picture the best image growing larger until it takes over the entire screen.

Suggestion

"Everything about me looks better. My hair is just right. My clothes are becoming. I am neat and clean. I am filled with pride at my fine appearance."

APTITUDE...

Hypnosis can reveal abilities the subconscious tends to conceal. Search the warehouse of the mind for basic creative instincts and natural abilities, which have been lying dormant.

Imagery

In a medium or deeper level, see the wide open sky. a sky-writing plane is practicing. Ask your question and watch as the plane writes out the answer across the sky. Imagine the message becoming smaller and smaller until it forms a stream of energy, comes down from the heaven and seeps into your mind.

Suggestion

"I will explore all possibilities to discover my strongest aptitude. I will then pursue it for an expanded life with abundant success."

AQUAPHOBIA...

Fear of deep water is a common problem, especially for people who were forced to swim as children. In extreme cases, victims will not travel overseas on ships, or even get into a small canoe.

Imagery

You are strolling in the country on a summer day. You see before you a warm, clean, shallow lake. You stand and see your reflection in the water. You are calm, smiling; you are confident. You walk into the water. It is soothing to your skin. You float in the water without conscious effort. It feels so good.

Suggestion

"Being in water is natural. All life comes from water. I enjoy letting it caress my body with it's little ripples. I can move around in it, safely."

AUTO-SUGGESTION...

Auto-suggestions are self-commands. Which can propel the mind and body to move in the right direction. They are the activators that bring about all affirmative improvements.

Imagery

See yourself at a social gathering where there are gossips. You overhear the onslaught of verbal attacks and put-downs and your own name is mentioned in a sarcastic way. See yourself as an assertive person.

Suggestion

"I am constantly on guard against negative remarks from other people. When I hear them, I counteract by telling myself positive auto-suggestions."

AROMATHERAPY...

After inducing a light state of hypnosis, an herbal or flower essence is passed over the face of the subject, by the hypnotist. A positive suggestion is given for deepening the trance and accepting the reconditioning program, which the subject has worked out in advance.

Imagery

You are leisurely walking in the country on a beautiful day. You see a garden of aromatic flowers. You enter the garden and your senses rejoice as you see the colors and smell the various aromas. You hear music, and a wave of happiness flows and glows through every cell of your body.

Suggestion

"I will increase my sense of well-being and enjoy my sensuality in every way. My perfect sight. Sense of smell. My hearing, and my touch. I enjoy tasting healthy food. Life is beautiful. I seize each moment as a joyful gift."

ARTHRITIS PAIN...

The number of people in the United States, afflicted with this condition, has been estimated at 37 million. Sufferers report relief of pain with hypnotic suggestion while in a trance level. One's breathing exhalation is directed to the point of greatest discomfort as an exit.

Imagery

Picture the troubled body part as very active. See it before the problem existed. Picture a blackboard. Write on the blackboard: "What caused the problem, in the first place?" Erase your question and watch the blackboard give you an answer.

Suggestion

"Each time I practice pain exhalation, I develop increased flexibility and comfort. I will do whatever is necessary to eliminate the problem. I will stick to a sensible exercise routine, keep my weight at the right level, and be disciplined in my choice of food."

ARTWORK...

You can greatly improve your work, by expanding your skills and talent through the self-hypnosis technique of "Rehearsal- Visualization."

Imagery

Once you have entered your creative CORE, imagine a blank canvass. See the painting in progress. Stand back and contemplate some additional improvements. See yourself making the changes. Sign your name.

Suggestion

"My work is getting better and better. I see the finished piece mentally, and simply follow through with the actualization."

ASSERTIVENESS TRAINING...

Inhibited people can learn to express themselves in an honest, direct, self-enhancing manner to ensure greater respect.

Imagery

Picture yourself standing in line at the post office. Someone tries to push in front of you. With good manners, you remind the person that you are in the right place. Next, see yourself standing in front of a blackboard chalk in one hand and eraser in the other. Write and erase the following:

Suggestion

"I will stand up for my rights and by doing so, gain admiration and respect from others.

1. I have the right to be wrong, any time.
2. The right to change my mind if I wish.
3. To be independent of other's suggestions.
4. To be illogical in making my own decisions.
5. To say "I don't understand what you mean."
6. Also: "No. I don't agree with your opinion."

ATTENTION DEFICIT DISORDER (ADD)...

As many as ten million people have this condition. While many adults live with this problem, it can be helped. It is the most common of all psychological disorders. Labeling a child as deficient can be a cop-out. The cause may be our teaching methods. Instead of helping children who are restless, we may be boring them with routine.

Imagery

Picture yourself concentrating on a jigsaw puzzle that will turn out to be a portrait of yourself as a contented person. As you focus on each piece you figure out where to place it, till you have completed the smiling picture of yourself.

Suggestion

"I will keep my mind focused on what I am doing or learning. If another thought tries to push its way into my attention, I will evict it and pay attention to what I have to."

AUDITIONS...

For performers. Actors, singers, musicians and dancers can perform at the highest level without anxiety. Also, for job interviews.

Imagery.

See a TV or movie screen. You are the performer, the director and the hiring agent. Create the results that you want to achieve. See yourself on the job.

Suggestion

"I am fully trained and capable of doing this work perfectly. My confidence is high and I am focused for success. I want it. I deserve it. I've got it."

AWKWARDNESS...

Feeling ill-at-ease reflects in the image presented to others. It shows lack of self-esteem. Human personality is made up of a collection of reflex habits. All of our activities center around these patterns. In order for you to overcome awkwardness, notice your entrenched habits and keep asking yourself, "Is this action helping me get where I want to go, or is it hindering me?"

Imagery

See yourself as you wish to be — calm and completely coordinated. You are balanced, in harmony with your environment and comfortable in the company of others.

Suggestion

"I can carry through any task properly. I train my body to be sure-footed and move gracefully."

BACK PAIN...

Five million Americans suffer from back problems and can be helped with hypnosis, either self-induced or with a therapist. Most cases have a contributing mental/emotional component. Check with a doctor to discover if the pain is organic, or due to tension. Lower stress and you may lessen the pain.

Imagery

See yourself waking up in the morning with a smile. You stretch out like a cat after a nap. Stand up, lift arms overhead, look into a mirror and say out loud, in a strong, commanding voice:

Suggestion

"The pain is gone and will not return. I am flexible mentally, and physically. I do whatever is necessary, so that the pain will go and never come back."

BARBITURATE DEPENDENCY...

People who use self-hypnosis learn that sedatives are unnecessary. Instead, they practice self-sedation, naturally. With self-hypnosis they use mental persuasion. It not only works well, but there are no side-effects.

Imagery

Stroll in the country, on a beautiful day. Become aware of your senses. Smell the flowers. Admire the variety of color. Hear your favorite meditation music. Now see a hammock between two trees. Get into the hammock and let the breeze rock your body into a state of bliss. As you meditate say to yourself:

Suggestion

"I have everything I need within myself to feel relaxed and contented under any conditions. Other people will not disturb me. I will transcend stress."

BASKETBALL EXPERTISE...

'Psyching-Up' is the secret ingredient that makes sports people into celebrities. Mind power is the secret ingredient behind the brilliant playing of slam-dunk stars, who appear to exceed any normal expectations.

Imagery

The subject enters a light trance and visualizes a television game, in which he stars, resulting in a dramatic win by his team. He sees the excitement of the crowd, and the gratitude and love of his team.

Suggestion

"Every time I play, I get better and better. I have everything I need to make it to the top. I can. I will and I must reach my potential."

BATTLE FATIGUE.

Combat soldiers who have been shocked mentally or physically are able to get back to a normal life by detaching themselves from the trauma. The best technique is to replace the automatic reflex of negative memory, by training the subconscious to have a new reaction to old stimuli.

Imagery

See yourself standing in front of a mirror, admiring your strong reflection-- shoulders back, head held high, smiling and confident. Remain in the trance visualization, and open your eyes.

Suggestion

Speak your suggestions out loud, while staring into your eyes. "I have learned lessons of survival from my experiences, I an more centered and balanced."

BEREAVEMENT...

A sense of continuous sadness and despair at losing a loved one, can be diminished by introspective light hypnosis. Using hypnosis in a group setting is comforting to people who find solace by interacting with others who have lived through a similar experience.

Imagery

Visualization takes on a spiritual quality as the departed person is seen as a spirit-guide advising the subject to live a fulfilling life with high values.

Suggestion

"I am thankful for all the good things I have learned from the relationship and will cherish the memories."

BESTIALITY...

A form of sexual aberration, where people practice sexual intercourse with animals. This may also refer to brutish behavior. This inhuman self-image can prod the victim to behave in anti-social ways, such as rape, molestation and violence.

Imagery

This requires a skilled therapist with knowledge of spiritual hypnosis. Therapist: "Visualize yourself inside a spiritual temple with a golden light shining down upon you, through a crystal dome at the top. The light forms a penetrating laser beam which enters your mind to erase the place where the reflex is recorded. In it's place, imagine a humanistic attachment to a special person.

Suggestion

"I am no longer obsessed with attitude and action that are beneath my intelligence. I am worthy of being loved by a person of high standards and I will change in whatever way I need to for this to occur."

BRAIN-TRAINING...

Under hypnosis, positive programming is accepted by the cerebrum (conscious thought), then sent to the cerebellum (action center). Suggestion affects the thalamus and the brain stem, which is in charge of breathing, heartbeat and other automatic health functions. In addition, hypnotic therapy releases endorphins, a natural opiate, manufactured by the brain. This aids pain relief and well-being.

Imagery

Once you master self-hypnosis, practice this visualization when you are in bed, ready to fall asleep. Begin by scanning your body, starting with your feet and working up to your head. As you see a part of your body, improve it with your brain-power.

Suggestion

"Brain, keep each part of me healthy, youthful, and free from problems. Send your natural healing substances, wherever I need help."

BREAST ENHANCEMENT...

There have been some positive results in breast enlargement for women from nineteen years to thirty-five, based on trance-visualization. A report, by the American Society of Psychosomatic Medicine, states that the stimulation of breast growth stems from the suggested increase of blood circulation and estrogen hormones. The increase in the test group ranged from .75 inches to 2.75 inches, in eight weeks.

Imagery

Visualization combines expanded breathing while in the medium trance level. See yourself inhaling through your nostrils and release the breath out through the nipples. As you exhale see the breasts as you wish them to be. Be realistic. Results are responsive to the self-fulfilling prophecy which states: Conceive and Believe if you wish to Achieve.

Suggestion

"Each and every time I take a deep breath, whether I am meditating in an hypnotic trance or awake, I will be activating healthy circulation and encouraging the normal enlargement of my breast."

BREAST FEEDING...

Because emotions impact on the glandular system, lactating women who practice self-hypnosis say that they are able to maximize the amount and quality of mother's milk.

Imagery

During pregnancy and after, close your eyes and picture the loving child nursing at your full breast with a look of contentment and love. The baby smiles and pats the breast, affectionately.

Suggestion

"I am healthy and normal in every way. Nursing my baby is a natural pleasure that soothes my nerves and bonds me with my offspring. Our love grows as the milk flows."

BLADDER CONTROL...

Incontinence is a symptom, not a disease. The urgent need to pass urine, is often due to stress, either of a physical nature such as coughing or sneezing, or a nervous, emotional reaction to a certain situation. Before embarking on a hypnosis solution, see your physician for an examination.

Imagery

Visualize yourself at your doctor's office. He is telling you that you do not have a serious disease, and can overcome your nervousness and incontinence.

Suggestion

"I can always sense the need to urinate in advance, so there is time to relieve myself in an appropriate way. Every day I notice improvement. I will get on with my life because the old problem has disappeared".

BLEEDING...

People who have difficulty controlling excessive bleeding from accident or surgery, report being helped from hypnotic suggestion. There are instances where hemophiliacs have lessened the problem, also. Both hetero-hypnosis and self-hypnosis are dramatically effective

Imagery

Diminishing bleeding begins with a deep trance level, and visualization is centered on the final cessation of the problem. Suggestion and deepening is combined. Depth is reached, by repetitive countdowns, such as:

Suggestion

"When I count down from twenty to zero, the bleeding will diminish with each count, and when I reach zero, it will stop altogether."

BLOOD PRESSURE...

Fifty million Americans suffer from elevated pressure. Scientists have established that moods and behavior can raise or lower blood pressure. Corrective measures include exercise, choice of foods and mental/emotional stress management. Hypnotic color-visualization is very helpful. Tests done at the University of Alberta, Canada lowered pressure by using color visualizations, as follows:

Imagery

Green had moderately good power, blue much better, and black showed the greatest results. Here is an example of color therapy combined with hypnosis to lower both systolic and diastolic levels: See yourself floating in a boat on a lake with beautiful green trees all around. You look up into the clear blue sky and feel a wave of serenity flow over your body. Now the boatsman takes you and the boat into a small dark cave where the walls are covered in black velvet. You see a chart, and on the chart, picture the results of your meditation. See the corrected numbers.

Suggestion
"My blood pressure is now in the normal range and will stay that way. I am free of stress and outside pressures, because I am calm on the inside."

BODYBUILDING...
If you don't care for your body, no one else will. The best time to start is when you still have a choice. Many body-builders psyche themselves up with self-hypnosis. It helps them lift more weight then they would, ordinarily.

Imagery
See yourself in great shape — the best that you can be. You are on stage at a contest for Mr. Universe. You are being applauded for your poses. Imagine winning the prize as everyone cheers.

Suggestion
"I will keep in shape always, and have increased energy for all activities. I feel like a winner. I look like a winner, and I can only become better."

BOWLING SKILL..
Hypnosis has turned out to be a hit with league bowlers and beginners. The ball will never go into the gutter, if you are focused into a light hypnosis (Alpha state) eyes-open concentration.

Imagery
Picture yourself as you step up to the line. You are holding the ball correctly. You are balanced. You have assumed the proper stance. Eyes firmly fixed on the pins. You release the ball as you keep your eyes straight ahead, visualizing all pins struck down.

Suggestion

"Each time I go bowling, my confidence increases more and more, and my SCORE improves. I will not allow anyone to distract me or interfere with my focus."

BRAINWASHING...

When painful visions from the past consume the subject's mind, sometime the only recourse is to cleanse the space and replace it with new programming. This only works with the subject's approval and participation.

Imagery

Cleansing the brain of toxins and negative impressions requires a system of accelerated breathing. The brain is only two percent of your body weight yet uses forty percent of your oxygen and affects all body functions. Picture the air coming in through the right ear, flowing through the right brain, where it picks up the garbage and blows it out the left ear.

Suggestion

"With every breath, awake or asleep, I eliminate the negative images and replace them with positive ones."

BRUXISM...

This refers to the grinding of teeth and can cause serious dental problems. This takes place during the night. This unconscious reflex may be due to repressed anger of a strong desire to strike back. Fear of releasing this strong emotion and being punished, is trapped in the jaw muscles..

Imagery

Picture yourself fast asleep and dreaming of resolving the conflict, with amiable compromise. See your face contented and smiling. Deliberately exhale each breath through your cheek muscles as you focus on the following suggestions:

Suggestion

"I am fearless and free of all negative anger and repression. I will express my opinions in a constructive way and stand up for my rights."

BULIMIA...

The habit of overeating and then throwing up, often stems from insecurity about being loved and accepted. The overeating may be a way to compensate and the throwing up is punishment to self for being unworthy of love and/or lack of perfection.

Imagery

To improve one's self image, the mirror method works very well. See yourself at your proper weight. Your skin is clear and radiant. You are fully energetic.

Suggestion

"I will stick to a healthy, low calorie diet and feel full and satisfied without overeating, so I never need to throw-up. The habit is unhealthy and disgusting. I am worthy of a better self-image."

BURN INJURIES...

In addition to relieving pain and promoting rapid healing, hypnosis imagery brings hope and courage to overcome memories of the trauma. Both Regression and Progression techniques are useful. Imagery encourages possibility thinking that one can recover and improve rapidly, without scar tissue.

Imagery

The vision begins by seeing a split screen. On one side picture a calendar, seeing pages flipping forward day by day. The other half of the screen shows the burned area becoming better day by day. As you reach a goal date, see yourself restored to normal.

Suggestion

"I have great healing power. My brain reduces pain and send messages to the cells, to improve rapidly. My attitude is positive. I expect the best."

BURN-OUT...

Emotional and physical exhaustion from overwork can be changed to high energy. Hypnosis allows you to work smarter, not harder. You can plan and organize your time. Your productivity will be enhanced with less effort.

Imagery

See yourself with awareness. What are you doing that is expending more energy than necessary? Recall a past event that drained you, and then focus on correcting your reaction to it. See yourself practicing calmness.

Suggestion

"I will avoid becoming too emotionally involved. I will take whatever happens in stride and remain calm and centered. I will live in the moment without stress or worry."

BUSINESS ACUMEN...

Hypnotic meditation is a means of sharpening judgment in making the right decisions. Also, the quality of work and financial reward will escalate, dramatically, if one practices regularly.

Imagery

The Brain-Computer Technique is suitable here. In a medium trance level, picture the monitor of your computer. Select SEARCH and enter a question. You are tapping into your higher intelligence for the answer. See it appear on your mental monitor.

Suggestion

"I will explore the central CORE of each issue and make the right choices. I will remain free of stress, no matter how busy my schedule. I will meet my goals and manage people with expertise."

CAFFEINE DEPENDENCY...

No need for a toxic boost with its ups and downs, emotionally. You can achieve better results with your own mind power and drinking healthier beverages. The process of change begins with cutting down the quantity of consumption to one or two cups a day. Then to a decaffeinated brand. From then, if the motivation is strong enough, you can switch to an herbal tea.

Imagery

You are having lunch in your favorite bistro. Though other people are ordering and drinking coffee, you stick to your resolve, and order what is best for you. You are not influenced by other people weak choices.

Suggestion
"I am following a healthy routine. I feel satisfied without caffeine, whether that is in a cold drink or a hot one."

CANCER...
The influence of one's mental attitude, and expectations are major forces in remission and cure, as well as prevention. After you succeed in placing yourself in a light to medium trance, feel healing energy flow to your area of affliction and see that part of you radiate light. Our bodies are constantly building new cells to replace the damaged ones.

Imagery
Visualize that life-giving power surround and consume your illness. Dr. Carl Simonton's method has proven very successful. Here's how it works: Visualize your bloodstream. See your white cells as rugged "Knights in Armor", indestructible. They fight the nasty intruders who are vanquished and destroyed. The enemy cancer cells give way to the power of the conquerors. See your specific condition changing for the better. As the evil forces leave you, drift into a pure atmosphere, where you are immune to all problems.

Suggestion
"My healthy blood cells have conquered the bad enemy invaders. I see improvement right now and expect more each day. I am aware of my own healing power and will use it effectively."

CAREER TRANSITIONS...
Making a move to another situation or moving up the ladder, because of a promotion, all bring butterflies to the stomach of the person with insufficient self-confidence.

Imagery
This calls for the "Rehearsal Technique," which means to practice in your mind, before you go through the actual physical changes. See yourself seated in

a movie house, watching the screen, as you enjoy your success in the new career position.

Suggestion
"I am ready and able to step up the ladder to a higher paying position. It will be easy for me to do because I am trained and capable in very way."

CARPAL TUNNEL SYNDROME...
In the case of painful muscle-joint disorders, hypnosis acts as a muscle relaxant, For those clients who are deep-CORE subjects it can remove pain symptoms entirely.

Imagery
Practice "Screen of the Subconscious." You see a movie of yourself, moving backward in reverse. The images regress you to a time before you had the disorder. See yourself using both hands and arm muscles, without strain or pain.

Suggestion
"The pain lessens each time I practice hypnosis. I keep the image before me of how my arms and wrists were before. The problem is diminishing and soon will be gone permanently."

CHILD ABUSE...
Each year over three million kids are mistreated, usually by their own families. They are punched, slapped, kicked or struck with hard objects by uneducated and frustrated adults. This usually leaves scars on the personality, as well as the body..

Imagery
"With regression, revisit the scenes in your childhood, when and where the trauma took place. Only this time reverse the roles of the abuser and the abused. Picture yourself as fully grown, and the abuser as the size you were when it happened. Now you are the authority figure and the other person is subservient. Instead of acting abusive you sit the smaller person

down and give him/her a good talking to, explaining the appropriate way to train children".

Suggestion

"I am now fully mature and understand the limitation of those that were unable to behave properly due to their ignorance and lack of sensitivity."

CHILDBIRTH...

Contractions, the first stage of childbirth, is called labor. This is because it is expected to be hard work. However, it doesn't have to be as bad as some women anticipate, if they have been trained to get into an altered state of mind.

Imagery

Visualize the baby moving into position. Accept the pressure as natural. It may feel like you may have a bowel movement. That's okay. You breath deeply through the pelvic area. Contractions make you feel happy because the baby is ready to come out. Imagine holding a beautiful baby who will enrich your life.

Suggestion

"I am an animal. I will let go and flow with mother nature's vibrations. My breathing is strong. I emphasis the exhalation. This causes my lower muscles to relax. The cervix to opening wide, a doorway to a new life."

(After Delivery)

"I am healthy and free of all birthing problems. My normal look returns rapidly. My weight is back where it should be. I have high energy and will nurse without difficulty and enjoy the wonders of this miraculous experience."

CHOLESTEROL REDUCTION...

In addition to whatever medication is prescribed, a strong dose of positive thinking and profound relaxation helps. Hypnosis also is useful to stick to the prescribed special diet.

Imagery

You are at your doctor's office. He hands you a print-out of your last blood test.

He is smiling. Your cholesterol has dropped down to the normal range. Now you are both smiling and shaking hands.

Suggestion

"I will stick to my prudent lifestyle, exercise and eat properly. I will transcend tension and keep my emotions cheerful."

CLAUSTROPHOBIA...

Anxiety about being in closed-in areas, such as elevators, closets, etc. This stems from childhood experiences and can be corrected by regression techniques to the time of the original trauma. There are several visualizations that work. The following is my favorite:

Imagery

Age regression, under the guidance of a professional hypnotist is indicated here. The subject is instructed to raise his/her forefinger to indicate the year that the first sense of fear manifested itself. When that is determined, the therapist tells the subject to imagine standing under a waterfall on a warm, summer day. The cleansing spray enters the top of the head and sprays out through the eyes the nose, the lips, and ears. A major cleansing is going on.

Suggestion

"I an growing less anxious about closed in areas. I wake up every morning, raring to go — to see new places and new faces."

COCAINE...

The most serious problem associated with snorting cocaine, is that there is a neurological reaction that ricochets inside the skull, rearranging the reality of the mind. Prolonged addiction can make this kind of person dangerous to self and others, because reality and fantasy become intertwined.

Imagery

If the addiction is of long standing, it usually requires a hypnotist, who uses the "Split-Screen" method. One side features the worst results from the addiction — the bleeding nose, etc. The positive image takes command and expands to push the addicted image off the screen.

Suggestion

"I am independent of quick-fixes and from now on, I look within my self for natural gratification."

COLDSORES...

Chronic crusted sores on the lips can be avoided by mind-control, directed toward healing the injured cells. Get into the trance as soon as possible after the first sign of a symptom. The suggestions work best at bedtime.

Imagery

Use the mirror technique after entering the medium trance level. See the blemish growing smaller and smaller, as you speak out loud into your reflection:

Suggestion

"I don't want this to happen ever again. When I awaken in the morning and look into this mirror the sore spot will be gone and never ever return."

CONDOM TOLERANCE...

The correct use of a condom could help cut the venereal disease statistics in half. Reluctance is based on the lessening of sensation. However, hypnotic suggestion, can actually increase sensation for both man and woman. Entering the light, hypnoidal level during foreplay has proved effective.

Imagery

See the action of putting on the protective shield, by the woman or the man. They communicate about the device making the feeling stronger for both of them

Suggestion

"Every time I feel the sensation of the rubber stimulating my pleasure nerves, I become more aroused. The condom is like an extra skin, adding friction to intercourse. Sex is better and better with a condom."

COLITIS...

Because bowel disturbances like bloating, cramping and diarrhea, are intensified by anxiety. Therefore, hypnosis becomes nature's antidote to correct the problem, permanently. A balanced diet with an abundance of fiber is the choice of many health practitioners.

Imagery

Picture yourself at a health club, going through your routine of simple exercise, waking up muscle tone in the abdominal region. This stimulates the internal organs into doing a better job. Also, imagine a coating of healing protection being applied to the inner organs, making them impervious to problems.

Suggestion

"I am noticing an improvement every day. I will stick to a discipline health routine and stay free from the problem of colitis."

COMPUTER LEARNING.

Focusing attention on methodology in computer learning takes persistent concentration. Only a light state of self-hypnosis is necessary to clear the way for creative use of the miracles that present themselves with knowledge of the computer.

Imagery

You are seated at the computer after first reading through the manual of instructions. You apply to the keyboard what you have just learned from the manual. Your concentration and focus have been sharpened. Your mind is keenly aware and you are ready to apply the new information you have learned.

Suggestion

"I will read, learn and apply the knowledge. Anything anyone else can do, I can do, also. I will be patient and be able to use my computer to advance my goals."

CONCENTRATION...

Concentration is the ability to shut out disturbances to focus on a central idea.

Hypnosis has a stunning affect in all areas where concentration is needed — work, learning, etc. Emptying the mind of extraneous thoughts, and focusing on the new suggestions, makes them become a reality, sooner.

Imagery

See yourself standing at a blackboard, you have a chalk in one hand and an erasure in the other. You are going to write and erase each letter of the alphabet, from A to Z, slowly and methodically. Even though other thoughts might try to filter into your mind, you immediately go back to the visualization being worked on.

Suggestion

"I have disciplined thinking. When I put my mind to a task, all other thoughts are set aside. Improved concentration will improve my life in every way."

CONDITIONING...

Humans have been subliminally trained to self-destruct. Our culture makes us prey to mercenary interests. We are programmed by advertising which cuts the human life span by 10 to 20 years. The average person is not even aware of these suggestions. Like sheep, masses of people amble on to their own slaughter, due to indirect media conditioning.

Imagery

Picture yourself holding the remote control and shutting off commercials that you do not choose to be conditioned by. Visualize a cartoon of a brain being invaded by an enemy force and fighting it off.

Suggestion

"I am independent of other people's programming. I will only do what is healthy and appropriate for my best interests."

COORDINATION...

Proper functioning of the neuro-transmitters of organs, muscles, and nerves, begins in the brain, which responds to hypnosis and the power of creative imagination and persuasive suggestion.

Imagery

Visualize yourself in a class doing some form of martial art, where balance and coordination is essential. See yourself in slow-motion and notice how skilled your reflexes are. You are an example of how dedicated practice builds skill. The class applauds your improvement.

Suggestion

"I have the ability to improve with consistent practice. My brain and body are normal in every way."

COSMETIC SURGERY.

Improving face and/or body is more likely to turn out the way you want it, if the mind is in a cooperative mood. There will be less pain and bruising if you prepare for the best results.

Imagery

Picture yourself performing some television magic. You are holding a remote control device with which you can change a photo of yourself. Make all the alterations you wish, until you are fully pleased.

Suggestion

"I know what I want and the results will be even better than I anticipate. I will be an easy patient and inspire my doctor to do a superb job."

CONSTIPATION...

Self-hypnosis is the best technique to employ. It is natural to have one to three bowel movements each day. Regularity can make a healthy difference in life. Eliminate toxic waste from your body by combining high fiber diet (lots of vegetables) with water, juices, exercise and most important, train your digestive system to avoid congestion.

Imagery

Picture yourself relaxed, sitting on the toilet seat and feeling the urge to evacuate take over. It happens naturally and easily. The stools are soft moist and there is no strain. You stand up and flush a normal amount of excretion.

Suggestion

"My digestive system is functioning well. There is no tension in the muscles of my lower body. I will always eat properly and drink ample water to ensure pleasant, gentle and complete bowel movements."

CONTACT-LENS COMFORT...

For those with sensitivity to the insertion of the lens onto the surface of the eye, visualization of blending with the contours of the eyes receptive surface brings comfortable acceptance.

Imagery

Picture yourself looking into a wall mirror, as you prepare a contact lens for insertion. See yourself apply the fluid in one easy motion. Then slip it onto the surface of the eye and blink. Smile at yourself.

Suggestion

"I have become accustomed to the feeling. It is as if the contact lens is my own flesh, a perfect fit, to give me perfect sight."

CREATIVITY...

Invention emanates from intuition of inspired minds in an hypnotic state. Of all human endeavors, the visual arts and composition of music, play an important role for human progress. The Alpha state has led to many of today's electronic and artistic accomplishments.

Imagery

Internalized visualization is attained by intense focusing. If you wish to have a preview of your success creatively, picture an art gallery with a large turn out of people interested in your work. If music, picture yourself at a concert, where they are playing your music. Imagine the applause.

Suggestion

"Whenever I so choose, I will return to my trance state to enhance my artistic talent. I will succeed, because I have everything that it takes to be recognized and appreciated."

CULT DEPROGRAMMING...

Misguided followers of self-serving leaders are often people who lack sufficient self-esteem and fall into rank behind someone who uses their time energy and money. Often they are brain-washed into believing they need a charismatic leader to make their life meaningful. Here's how to gain freedom from entrapment.

Imagery

The first step is to discover why the victim made this choice. The blackboard technique works by asking questions of the subconscious mind, such as:

> What was missing in my life?
>
> How can I become my highest self?

Next picture yourself at the wheel of a bus whose destination is marked "Self Fulfillment"

Suggestion

"I am at the steering wheel, in the drivers seat of my life. I know where I'm going and I know how to get there. If it is going to be, it is up to me."

CYBERSPACE-STRESS...

Computers have made robots out of people who are trapped in the binds of technology. This can only escalate in the new century as inventors develop even more technology. Plugging into the Internet, participants join an imaginary universe, with fantasy people, who often present themselves in less than honest ways.

Imagery

See yourself at a celebration where all of your dearest friends and family members are rejoicing. See the hugging and kissing and the emotionally exchange of good feeling. The realization that human interaction is gratifying and that involving in

Suggestion

"No matter how absorbed I become in the Internet and all of its ramifications, I will enjoy human interaction, and the pleasure of socializing."

DANCING...

If you've tried to learn and felt like you had two left feet, hypnosis can bring you a sense of balance, build confidence, and relaxation to feel inspired by the rhythm of the music.

Imagery

This is a fun visualization. Imagine a movie of the finest professional dancer, that you especially admire. and place your face on the dancer's body.

Suggestion

"Each time that I picture myself dancing, I become more confident. I have everything it takes to improve with practice."

DEAF-MUTE TECHNIQUE...

Tactile hypnosis (by touch) is extremely effective for the deaf and hard of hearing. First they watch a demonstration of a hearing person being hypnotized so they know the process. Then, they are given a card, upon which they write their personal auto-suggestions. Visual charts explain each step before induction: "Concentrate on what you have written on your card. Another sign is shown: "Each time I touch your shoulder, go deeper." Another sign: "When I tap both shoulders, open your eyes and remain in a trance to read your suggestions "

Imagery

As soon as the subject's eyes are closed, they are creating their own images. Next, the practitioner taps the subject's shoulder to go deeper. Taps on both shoulders signal: "Open your eyes."

Suggestion

With open-eyes, they now gaze on their cards and/or charts, with suggestions for improvement, as well as post-hypnotic suggestions.

DENTAL PAIN REDUCTION...

No shots. Self-induced comfort, anesthesia, pain free, needle-free, and chemical free. There is a higher level of personal trust throughout the procedure. Also, the dentist gets more done.

Imagery
Patient is relaxed to eliminate tension and fear of pain, then told to imagine he/she is at the top of a winding staircase and to count the steps on the way down, starting with 100 until reaching zero.

Suggestion
Given by dentist; "As you descend the staircase the pain is goes down. When you get to zero, there will be no pain at all. Instead, you will feel very happy and look forward to some happy news. Imagine you are home. The phone ring and you get into a nice, long conversation about good things happening."

DENTURE COMFORT...
Don't throw away your plates, or your braces — there's hope. The use of hypnosis in orthodontics has been successfully practiced for over fifty years. The comfort and acceptance of prosthetic devices by the patient, depends on their ability to imagine the appliance as natural and comfortable.

Imagery
After leaving the dentist's office, use the power of your mind to assist in the successful changes. Visualize eating an apple with gusto and feeling like the dentures are your original teeth.

Suggestion
"The dental work and the device that I must wear improve my appearance dramatically. I will become accustomed to the feeling, quickly."

DEPRESSION...
The inability to function due to unhappy thoughts is self-perpetuating. Because it is self-inflicted, it can be self-erased and replaced by a better emotional state of mind. Hopelessness and helplessness vanish with this meditation:

Imagery
After reaching trance level, visualize yourself answering the phone. You receive great news. Something you have wanted for a long time. See your self smiling and cheering, you are ready to unburden your depression now. To clear out old

imbedded negativism, suggestions must be planned and repeated often. An audio tape made by a professional, can speed the recovery.

Suggestion

"I have an increased feeling of well-being, of energy and expanded creativity. I think positive thoughts. Abundant hope takes over despair and inertia."

DETOXIFICATION...

People who are out of control, resort to a puff of smoke; a toke of pot, a snort of cocaine. Why do some people fall into the thrall of addictive substances, while others wouldn't consider damaging themselves? The difference in these two types of people is, the user seeks a fix from outside, the non-user reaches inwardly to natural resources.

Imagery

The detox process is most effective when using the water technique. You are floating in a warm lake of cleansing water, that is shallow and safe. A divine white light is shining down upon you, from above. Imagine that you are a large sponge, sponge in water, light and oxygen and squeeze out the poisons.

Suggestion

"I am voiding my body of parasites, drugs, alcohol and all side effects. I will drink lots of water and other liquids, and cleanse noxious thoughts from my mind."

DIABETIC DIET DISCIPLINE...

Without some form of mind — control, diabetics have difficulty maintaining their very strict diet. For some, this can be a matter of life or death. The most dependable method to maintain discipline, is learning the art of hypnosis.

Imagery

See yourself in your doctor's office. He is holding your chart, explaining to you the results of your latest tests. He is pleased. You are both smiling.

Suggestion

"I will follow my doctor's orders, and my health will keep improving. My weight is normal and my taste for sweets has diminished dramatically."

DISABLED JOB TRAINING...

Both the unemployed and the "unemployable" can realize their fullest potential by optimizing their capabilities. The first step toward improvement is to realize that a handicap is a state of mind. Physically challenged individuals find help in the power of the mind that not only eases physical strain and pain but also keeps their spirits high.

Imagery

You are standing and looking out of a glass window. This is the window of opportunity, which enlarges as you visualize how you can become more than you are. See yourself as enabled, rather than disabled.

Suggestion

"I have altered my state of awareness and proud of what I can do. I enjoy training to improve and have set goals for myself that I expect to reach."

DISLEXIA...

Hypnotic power helps to optimize the subject's concentration. There is a great deal of misdiagnosis in this area. Learning and using self-hypnosis is empowering to the afflicted person. Hypnosis will remove stress and anxiety and optimize the brains ability to overcome the limitations.

Imagery

See yourself absorbed in a book about a subject you are especially interested in. There are pictures as well as text and you find you are turning the pages more rapidly than you ever did before.

Suggestion

"Other people have overcome this condition and so will I, because I am intelligent and have the power to improve. I will take responsibility for changing."

DIVORCE...

Today, about sixty percent of all marriages end in divorce, with sexual incompatibility cited as a major cause. In the United States, over ninety percent of all patients who see psychiatrists and other analysts, do so because they are having relationship problems.

Imagery

Regress your mind to the first time you realized you were in love with your spouse. Recall the emotions, as well as the physical attraction. Remember the place and the conversation that first took place. Let the scene change to the breakup. Now ask your higher mind, "Where did I go wrong?" See the answer appear on your mental screen.

Suggestion

"I am learning from this experience and will do everything I can to correct my part of the problem. I will talk it through and try to make repairs. If that doesn't work, I will be a wiser person for my next relationship."

DREAM INTERPRETATION...

A dream is a window into one's secret world. As Freud said, "A dream is a message from the unconscious, and if not understood is like a letter left unopened. Hypnosis is an uncovering modality and not only retrieves the dream but also interprets the symbols and archetypes that the unconscious mind is expressing.

Imagery

The best time to recall a dream, is just before falling asleep, preferably the next night. When you enter the threshold of nighttime slumber, focus on remembering the past dream and ask your mind to reveal the meaning. It may appear on a screen, blackboard or in a cloud formation while you focus into the sky.

Suggestion

"Each and every time that I dream, I will increase my power to understand the meaning of the dream, and by so doing, improve my life."

DRUG DEPENDENCY...

Whether over the counter or under, drug addiction is the nation's No.1 health problem and cause of death. Researchers at Baltimore's John Hopkin's University report that opiates travel to a part of the brain which produces euphoria, causing dependency. Tranquilizers, energizers, sleeping pills, painkillers, appetite depressants and others, only remove symptoms. Hypnotic suggestion can do more; because it often erases the fundamental cause, such as stress and anxiety.

Imagery

Picture yourself radiating wellness, in a natural setting. You are strolling along on a beautiful day in the country. All of your senses expand your high euphoric feeling. This is the antidote to dependency.

Suggestion

"I will open my senses to enjoy being alive. My sense of sight to see beauty. My ears will hear singing. I will breath the aroma of nature, and hug my friends."

EATING DISORDERS...

A balanced diet is the single most important factor in maintaining a healthy body and mind. Bingeing. Purging. Starving. Vomiting. Food-dysfunctional people lead a life-and-death battle with appetite. However, they respond to hypnotic strategies with outstanding results because food addiction goes deeper than consciousness — to the autonomic reflex system. Humans are the only animals cursed with addicted appetite. Other animals eat to hunger. Health practitioners believe most human beings eat twice the amount necessary for health.

Imagery

Picture yourself standing in front of a full length three-way mirror. See yourself front view, back view and side view. Make all of the changes that you want for yourself. Slimmer here, firmer there. Notice a calendar on the wall with the goal-date for reaching your best image. Now get on a scale and weigh yourself. Notice that you have reached your goal. Imagine yourself working as a clothes model in the size that you prefer. The audience applauds.

Suggestion

"With every breath, I am full and satisfied without extra calories. I will follow the five point program for maintaining normal weight. 1..Postpone eating. 2..Choose low calorie foods. 3..Chew food very slowly.. Breath deeply to metabolize. 5.. Exercise frequently. 6.. Eliminate relapses.

ENERGENCY HELP...

Nurses and health care workers report the use of hypnosis as a useful adjunct to mouth to mouth resuscitation and other established methods. Hypnosis quiets the anxiety, and prepares the patient to cooperate fully.

Imagery

The health care worker describes recovery: "Just close your eyes and breath deeply. See your abdomen rising and falling with each breath. Picture yourself in great health, fully recovered."

Suggestion

Say to yourself "This emergency is past. I am back to my healthy self. Breathing increases my energy."

EMOTIONAL MATURITY...

Negative emotions begin early in life. The most powerful force is destructive criticism, inflicted on a child before the age of six. The memory bank stores this material. We have to reach into that warehouse to wash it away. Lack of unconditional love scars a child's psyche and the adult inner child craves compensation. People can and do improve at any age and at any stage of life. Maturity means you feel free to assert your need to share loving feeling.

Imagery

Regress to an age when you felt rejected or abandoned. Imagine that you are outside a window of a house you lived in as a child. As you observe a replay of your childhood, note the behavior of parents and family.

Suggestion

The following is based on the Menninger Institute's criteria for emotional maturity:

a...I can adjust to adverse conditions.
b...I am free from symptoms of tension/anxiety.
c...I am able to deal constructively with reality.
d...I get more pleasure from giving than receiving.
e...I relate to others, with mutual satisfaction.
f...I sublimate and direct hostile energy into creative, and constructive outlets.
g...I have the capacity to love others, rather than being self-centered.

ENURESIS (BED-WETTING)...

This is most common where children are concerned. The problem may be physical and/or psychogenic. With children, this is most often a manifestation of passive rebellion between child and parent. As such, it is treatable with hypnosis.

Imagery

Before the child falls asleep at night, describe this visualization: "Picture yourself fast asleep and smiling, contentedly. You see a clock over the bed and the hour hand moving steadily until the time you have to wake up. Now you awaken and find you are in a dry bed. You have slept all through the night, without wetting the bed. Now repeat after me:

Suggestion

"I will wake up in a clean dry bed. Before I go to sleep at night, I will go to the bathroom and sleep through the night dry until morning."

EPILEPSY...

This term is used to describe over twenty types of seizures which are chronic in nature. This means they happen periodically. The grand mal is the most serious and may cause the loss of consciousness. The less severe form is not long lasting and may be limited to facial muscles, with consciousness returning rapidly. Muscle spasms can be interrupted by a medical hypnotist and control taught to the patient. Self-hypnosis is the preferred modality, so the subject can, at a moment's notice, enter the trace level and stay balanced with normal awareness.

Imagery

Stress management lessens the severity of both types, and here the use of self-hypnosis can be extremely useful. At the first sign of possible seizure, the person taps into the brain's power to minimize the event. See the magic mirror and a smiling confident self. If you work at a computer, you might imagine these words appearing on the monitor: The feeling is just passing through. I will maintain my control.

Suggestion

"The problem is going and will be gone and never return. I have the power to overcome. My brain is sending out electrical signals to all my cells instructing them to diminish symptoms immediately."

EXHIBITIONISM...

The abnormal compulsion to expose one's body parts to strangers in order to attract salacious attention. Also, this term refers to the "show-off" personality, the topless dancer, etc. The extreme of this behavior is the "flasher," whose fetish prevents him from true intimacy. This psycho-sexual problem needs the help of a skilled therapist.

Imagery

Picture yourself involved in a caring-sharing relationship where there is mutual respect. See yourself as giving and receiving affection preceding physical intimacy.

Suggestion

"I have matured to a higher level. I have self-esteem and confidence to attract a lover, without resorting to inappropriate behavior."

FAITH ADDS POWER...

It has long been known that visualization without faith cannot bring about the achievement. Without a strong belief system, images only stir up wishful-thinking. When we have positive confidence in the outcome, we are motivated to go after wanted results. If you tell yourself that you can't make it, the belief is accepted and carried out. When you expect more of yourself, you deliver more.

Imagery

See a movie or TV screen and picture the title "Achieve Best Results". See yourself as the recipient of an award for your work and lifestyle.

Suggestion

"I can, I will and I must achieve what I want. I can conceive it and believe it and therefore I can and will achieve it."

FALSE MEMORY SYNDROME...

Memories of child abuse are often repressed and then recovered in detail by regressing during hypnosis. Some scientists are skeptical. They say memory is fragmented and prone to revision due to persuasion. Fortunately, validity can be ascertained in the altered state. This is done through automatic nerve reaction using finger signals. Here's how it works:

Imagery

The hypnotist uses age regression to the incident. Questions are asked, after informing the subject to raise the right finger if true, or the left finger if untrue. In cases where the memory is faulty, the subject's fingers will both tremble and signal the practitioner that the memory is triggered by imagination, or altered in some way.

Suggestion

"I will benefit from this experience. The truth will set me free to get on with my life and enjoy every moment, without bad memories, real or imagined ."

FASTING...

As a cleansing or spiritual meditation can be tolerated and even enjoyed in a state of mental tranquillity. It can flush your body and replenish your soul. However, it should be done with medical supervision or approval by your physician.

Imagery

The technique of "Positive Progression" is helpful here. If one see the successful completion of the healing fast, motivation is strengthened to stick to a health regime. A future directed mind-movie spurs one's incentive, during the fast period.

Suggestion

"I look forward to all the benefits from this fasting program. I am disciplined and prepared to continue a health pattern for the rest of my life."

FATIGUE...

A chronic tired feeling is not only the result of poor nutrition and limited oxygen, but is also, stress-related. Expand energy by opening up your lung capacity to add oxygen. Fatigue is relative to each individual's state of bodily fitness.

Imagery

Body awareness means an awakening to the total needs of one's physical self, by picturing all body systems in vigorous health. It is the knowledge that the body is a precious possession and perishable, if we allow it to perish. Good health demands coordination of all the interrelated systems of the body. These are:

1. The circulatory system
2. The respiratory system
3. The digestive system
4. The nervous system
5. The glandular system
6. The muscular system
7. The reproductive system

Suggestion

"I will maintain a strong self-image of strident health in every system of my body, internally and externally, mentally and emotionally."

FEAR OF FAILURE...

Fear is the root from which many distorted branches grow. Fears will always try to rear their ugly heads and must be slapped down with vigor. The average person's thinking is cluttered with blocks of apathy, skepticism, and fears. Fear will always try to rear it's ugly head and must be slapped down with vigor.

Imagery

See yourself in a situation that requires courage and some degree of risk-taking. See fear as a silly cartoon character. You are an enormous dinosaur with the power to slap down any foolish fear. Destroy, crumble and defeat the foolish fear image.

Suggestion

"My high self is free from fear-based limitations. I am zealous and determined to succeed in life and this means becoming fearless."

FEAR OF FLYING...

Aerophobia is often the result of an earlier experience which frightened the person. Imagery directed onto a screen revives the incident and a safe reenactment takes place subliminally, which later calms the conscious mind.

Imagery

Start conditioning a week or two before a flight. Record the therapy on an audio tape. This has proven to be successful. Many people take their recorder on the plane and play the tape during the flight. A post hypnotic suggestion is given to the subject, to the effect that the hypnosis training will be recalled as he steps into the plane

Suggestion

"I look forward to flying. I enjoy going to new places and seeing new faces. Every time I fly, I feel high and happy. As soon as I sit down in the plane, I will enter a calm state of mind."

FEMALE FRIGIDITY...

Over half of all woman surveyed, report that they have difficulty in achieving sufficient sensation to bring about a strong internal orgasm. When they depend solely on a man to arouse them, they often find themselves frustrated. Here's how to accelerate internal sensation.

Imagery

Picture yourself in an intimate embrace. Concentrate on the passage of oxygen coming in to the body through the nipples and passing down through the pelvic cavity in to the vaginal shaft. Focus on the "G" spot, located at the front (anterior) wall of the vagina. This light tingles and stimulates intense sensation which spreads from the inside to the outer labia and into the clitoris. Sensation pulsates from the outside into the inside — back and forth as you grow closer and closer to orgasm.

Suggestion

"I am sexually normal and have everything that it takes to respond fully. I enjoy penetration and look forward to more sensual feeling each and every time. I am free of guilt, shame and fear. My inhibitions are gone. I let myself go into the pleasure zone."

FETISHES...

A broad swath of the human population is dependent on using objects and/or unique situations to ensure their sexual function. Such people tend to be more aroused by objects than real, live people. The first step toward reaching fulfillment is to realize that you are free to make other choices and not limited or inhibited by dependence on anything.

Imagery

Visualize an erotic film in which you are the star. Your partner is perfectly matched to your desires. You are making love without the need for a fetish dependency, and it is even better than ever before.

Suggestion

"I am no longer dependent on a special object or situation to become sexually aroused. I will instead relate normally to an affectionate partner and build a more meaningful, erotic response."

FINANCIAL FREEDOM...

Those bound to mediocrity by having been born to poverty, can use their mental energy to guide them to economic security. It's all in the head. The first step is to see what you want. Use the law of the self-fulfilling prophecy...Conceive it. Believe it... And then... Achieve it.

Imagery

Let your mind fire up your motivation. Picture how you would live, if you had financial freedom right now. See the clothes you'd wear. The house you would live in and the car you would drive. Picture anything else that you would want if money was plentiful. Next, picture the blackboard. Chalk in one hand eraser in the other, you work out a plan.

Suggestion

"I have a plan, and know what needs to be done for financial freedom. Each day I will take steps to move closer to my goal. I know what I want and I know how to get it. If it's going to be, it is up to me."

GAGGING...

This presents a serious problem in dental work as well as the swallowing of pills and other medications. Some people gag when they eat and talk at the same time. A corrective action is to slow down and become aware of your breathing rhythms. Taking as low deep breath and swallowing only after exhalation.

Imagery

See yourself in a place and situation which might normally present anxiety and lead to gagging. Then imagine yourself free of the problem. Remember, as we see ourselves, we tend to become.

Suggestion

"The problem is gone and will not return. Any time in the future that I feel concerned, I will stop, think and overcome."

GAMBLING OBSESSION...

Thinking only in terms of being a winner or loser, spurs losers to try to become winners, even if the behavior is irrational. The consequences of gambling can be destructive. There are people who have lost their cars, homes and marriages. The underlying motivation of gamblers isn't just about money. Often it is connected to a lack of intimacy.

Imagery

Resistance to temptation comes in discovering the original trigger. The therapist regresses the subject to the situation which prompted the need to gamble. Finger signals are used to inform the practitioner when the proper age has been reached. Self-approved brain-washing works extremely well. The subject is told: "Imagine a waterfall a few inches above your head. As it flows into your skull and through your brain, the water releases all debris and obsolete gambling addiction. The water flows down through your body, out the soles of your feet and into the ground. The urge to gamble is gone permanently."

Suggestion

"I cannot depend on chance. I will, instead, choose to be more confident and self-sufficient. I can make my own luck, and become a real winner in life."

GASTROINTESTINAL DISCOMFORT...

Problems associated with food, such as bloating, diarrhea, cramps and irritable bowel syndrome, find remedial help through hypnosis. This is especially true when these conditions are stress related.

Imagery

This technique brings together the mind and body, while at the same time tapping the thought into the automatic motor system.

Suggestion

"I will remain calm and easy-going under all stressful conditions. Nothing is so important that it makes me feel sick. I will rise above annoyances."

GOAL ORIENTATION...

Both short term and long term goals require a plan, a map to guide you to your destination. Once you have set a rational goal for yourself, use hypnosis to motivate your striving. No matter how far you need to travel, every journey starts by taking the first step of planning. One step after the other leads you to your goals.

Imagery

Seeing is believing which makes the "Progression Technique" work like magic. It enables you to see into your future and anticipate what it will be like to reach your goals. The calendar is useful here. Set a date for reaching your goal and then see the day appear with actions taking place. The phone rings with good news. You receive mail, confirming success.

Suggestion

"Everything that must be done to reach my goal has been taken care of. I am disciplined and devoted to do the daily mundane tasks to achieve my aims."

HALITOSIS...

Chronic bad breath can be due to a variety of diseases and can be a symptom for diagnosis. In addition to seeing a doctor to make sure it is not organic, you can eliminate the emotional psychosomatic factor in the following way:

Imagery

Take yourself through the vision of walking in a lovely flower garden. Breathe in the aroma of your favorite flower and see the colored petals flowing out of your mouth. As you breathe in, you purify and as you breathe out you expel any unpleasant odor,

Suggestion

"I will choose the right foods that are easily digested without smelly side effects. I will use a breath freshener whenever I am in doubt."

HEADACHES...

Chronic headaches can be prevented and controlled. Whether a person suffers the cluster type or migraine, stress aggravates the condition and hypnotic meditation ameliorates it. Check with your physician and if all that your medication does is to remove symptoms, try self-hypnosis. Lowering stress can often remove the cause.

Imagery

Focused breathing reduces the congested feeling. Depending on the area which is most troubled, you imagine an opening about the size of a dime and you visualize blowing out the pain. If it is non-specific, imagine an opening at both sides of the temple, and as you breath out make a mantra sound of release: Ahhhmmmm.

Suggestion

"My head is cool and calm. My pulses are normal. I take everyday pressures in stride. No one and nothing that happens around me, can stress me out. The power of my mind has healed me."

HEALTHY HABITS...

There's a plethora of ailments which are correctable with the mind. Many unaware people are trapped in behavior which makes them sick and shortens their lives. Every time you think and every time you speak, you should know that each thought and word brings with it a physical reaction and a possible effect upon your body. There are literally hundreds of health problems that could be alleviated by the use of hypnosis.

Imagery

Magnetize cosmic healing by seeing a laser beam of spiritual light shine upon the area that needs cleansing. Feel the poisons leave your body as puffs of dark gray smoke. Use your senses to eject the debris. As the evil forces leave you, drift into an atmosphere where you are immune to all illness.

Suggestion

"Every day in every way, I become healthier and healthier. I follow a sensible health routine. I do the right thing to encourage my body to throw off all intrusions of illnesses. I think positive and make positive choices."

HEARING IMPROVEMENT...

Because the brain is so close to the receiving end of nature's hearing instrument, every word we say, or hear, can affect hearing loss. Human beings can distinguish between 300,000 to 400,000 variations of tonal vibrations. Here's how to improve yours: Before induction, place coins and dressmaker pins in a saucer near you so you can reach them when your eyes are closed.

Imagery

The act of hearing takes place when the motion of sound waves vibrates the inner ear, which is close to the brain. The inner ear is composed of a thin membrane stretched tautly over the end of a tunnel-like structure leading in from the outer ear. The sounds of words make this drum-like structure quiver its exciting messages to the brain; the brain in turn relays its answer to the entire nervous system.

Suggestion

As you drop the small metal objects on to a plate, say to yourself, "My hearing is improving as I concentrate on the sounds these objects make. Every time I practice my hearing gets better and better."

HEARTBURN/ACIDITY...

This discomfort associated with digestion is influenced by emotions or anger or frustration. Because of this factor, a state of prolonged relaxation is preventative. While antacids may neutralize the reflux problem temporarily, self-hypnosis will eliminate the cause.

Imagery

Start the visualization by seeing the blackboard upon which you can ask a question and receive an answer. Now, see yourself finishing up a nutritious meal.

Suggestion

"The heartburn is gone and will not return. I will choose the proper foods, eat slowly and remember to chew thoroughly, and drink plenty of water."

HEART HEALTH...

As stress escalates, maintaining a healthy heart becomes vitally important. Practicing regular self hypnosis can prevent stress-related cardiovascular disturbances. Most heart attacks happen early in the morning. Before jumping out of bed do 5 minutes. of hypnotic imaging.

Imagery

It helps to get an anatomy book so you can better relate to the function of any internal organ you are healing. See your heart in your mind's eye acting vigorous with all valves pumping normally.

Suggestion

"I eat well, treat my heart well, and my heart does the same for me — performing as nature intended."

HERPES BREAKOUTS...

The mind is powerful in the suppression of recurrence of this genital skin irritation. In addition to using techniques to speed healing, one can also avoid recurrence of outbreaks.

Imagery:

Use the mirror technique to see yourself as the world's healthiest person. Focus on your genitals, as radiantly free of the problem. Mentally remove any unwanted blemishes, sick cells, germs or toxins. See your healthy blood cells as a vast army of soldiers knocking out the enemy.

Suggestion:

"I am now invincible to outbreaks. I have built a shield of well-being around me. Herpes Is gone and will not return."

HICCUPS...

This is described as an involuntary spasmodic closure and opening of the glottis in the throat, producing a staccato sound. This problem may continue for weeks, or longer. People who are prone to have this disorder report that going into hypnosis can break the repetition of the annoying reflex.

Imagery

Visualize yourself as a tiny explorer, entering your mouth and traveling down your throat, searching for the hiccup impediment along the pathway. You come to a bump in the road and you smooth it out by massaging it with your hands as you say to yourself:

Suggestion
"My throat is smooth and free of interference. The hiccuping has stopped and will never return."

HOLISTIC HEALING...
Those of us who work in a holistic way to help medical doctors cure psychosomatic illness, understand the brain's connection to physical responses. We know that whenever a suggestion is repeated over and over again, it becomes a conditioned reflex and takes root in the autonomic nervous system.

Imagery
Symptoms differ, but the solution is the same — the power of imagination. Imagine yourself as your doctor's assistant. You are examining a medical monitor which shows the specific body part that needs correction. You type into your computer keyboard questions for correcting the condition, and then watch the monitor come up with the best solution.

Suggestion
"I have the power of mind-control over my body. Hypnosis is helping me to expedite the process of returning my body to healthy homeostasis."

HOMELESSNESS...
Is on the rise. Urban encampments of destitute people are rampant near bridges, freeways, railroad stations and wherever they can find some kind of shelter. A caring community can provide teaching skills and emotional support. Hypnotic group therapy has been effective in shelters where these people gather. It provides them with a tool for making changes in appearance and perception of themselves.

Imagery
Time regression method works best. Picture yourself as you were before your life got out of control. See yourself attending counseling and working out the best solutions instead of giving up.

Suggestion

"I have everything I need to live a normal life. I am in the driver's seat, rather than a wounded passenger in life. I will take action and my life will improve, one day at a time."

HUMOR...

Research shows that the average six year old laughs 300 times a day. However, the average adult only laughs zero to fifteen times. Over fifty percent are in the zero category. Studies have shown that people who are inclined to laugh and act merry, stay healthier and live a longer life-span. Attitude toward events in life are a major factor in freeing the spirit to soar to new heights.

Imagery

Use the movie theater technique. See yourself as a small happy child, sitting in the audience. The funniest movie you have ever seen is on the screen. Every one around you is laughing, and you are laughing the loudest. The vibrations of humor ripple through all your nerves.

Suggestion

"I will find something to laugh about every day. I will keep the happy child within me alive and well."

ILLITERACY...

One third of Americans who are teachable, can't read adequately. Hypnosis accelerates learning, especially in a group setting where peers encourage each other.

Imagery

Imagine that you are sitting in a library surrounded by people who are reading books. See yourself select a book of interest to you from one of the shelves. You join the other readers: they smile and you feel very happy. As you look at each printed word the meaning is clear to you. Tension and worry are gone.

Suggestion

"My confidence and comprehension become stronger with each word that I master. I have normal intelligence. I am free from anxiety."

IMAGINATION...

Albert Einstein said, "Imagination is more powerful than reality." It is the spark which ignites your power to reach your true potential. It is a necessary component of all creativity, music, art and science. Without it we would live like zombies.

Imagery

Picture a large artist's pad. You have a pencil in one hand, an eraser in the other. You can make a sketch for a painting, a sculpture, or write a poem or an idea for a script. If you're into music, jot down notes. This is your time to express your talent. The ideas will just flow from your glowing, radiant mind.

Suggestion

"Whenever I need to, I will enter my creative center and ideas will bubble out. I will never be at a loss for my imagination is powerful."

IMMUNE SYSTEM...

Hypnosis is a preventive measure that can enhance medical cure. This is because the mind directs the immune system. There is evidence that stress triggers the release of adrenaline, and other stress hormones, which suppress the immune system. Conversely a feeling of tranquillity can reverse the process. Molecules such as neuropeptides and their receptors link the brain to the immune system.

Imagery

Maximize healing by seeing a laser beam of spiritual light shine upon the area that needs cleansing. This is the divine light of the universe. Think of yourself as a sponge, all your pores open to receive the blissful healing. Feel the poisons leave your body. See them as puffs of dark gray smoke.

Suggestion

"Every day in every way, I become healthier and healthier. I follow a disciplined health routine. I do the right thing to encourage my body to throw off all intrusions of illnesses. Think positive and make positive choices."

IMPOTENCE...

Over ten million men, nationwide, admit to erectile dysfunction. The real figure might be double. Fortunately, most male potency problems can be corrected. Hypnosis is effective for the men who:

* Can get an erection only "some of the time"
* Can get only a partial erection (semi-soft)
* Tend to lose their erection inside the vagina
* Respond only under special, ideal conditions
* Respond only to certain women and not others

Imagery
Regressive visualization to a time of great virility, such as the teen-age years, often works to trick the nerves into a flow of sexual energy.

Suggestion
"I have everything I need to have healthy, normal sex. During foreplay, I will recall my most potent memory and that will spur my glands to function virally.

INTELLIGENCE (I.Q.)...

In an unstable world, only one thing remains constant — the human CORE of intelligence, This is unique in each of us and universal to all. You can boost your I.Q. up to ten point with hypnotic suggestion — and you can reinforce the improvement by yourself, with suggestion and music, while in a CORE trance...Theta state of mind.

Imagery
Lift your intelligence while in hypnosis as you simultaneously play melodic, classical music, such as Mozart or Debussey. As you relax and listen, visualize a chart with ascending numbers from one to ten. When you hear a musical phrase repeated, see the I.Q. marker go up a point. Keep listening.

Suggestion
"Each time I enter my trance center, with imagery and music, I will be recharging my brain's power to lift my intelligence to its highest potential."

INFIDELITY.

The inability to stay with one sexual partner can lead to a host of problems. In most cases changing partners does not get rid of the problem, but changing behavior does. Adding variety to intimacy works wonders to recapture the rapture that once was.

Imagery

Picture yourself in a passionate embrace with your devoted partner. It's more than animal sex, it's intimacy based on emotional interaction.

Suggestion

"I am capable of a mature, love relationship. It will satisfy me physically, emotionally and spiritually."

INFERTILITY TREATMENT.

As an assist to standard medical methods, hypnosis helps to maximize positive expectations that the sperm will actively pursue and impregnate the eager ovaries. When stress is lessened, conception has a better chance. This is true for both the male and the female.

Imagery

I have found the most effective way to insure a healthy, normal pregnancy is to have sexual intercourse while in the trance state. This can be achieved through mutual self-hypnosis, or by hypnotizing each other.

Suggestion

Every day in every way, I am more confident about this pregnancy. I adhere to a health routine. I am free oif anxiety. I am normal and ready for parenthood."

INSOMNIA...

A Gallup Poll revealed more than a third of Americans — 90 million people have sleep problems. Self-hypnosis training can ensure both restful nights and energetic days because hypnosis is the natural gateway to slumber.

Imagery

After total body relaxation, preceding the basic induction, monitored breathing is used as follows: Place your hands, palms down, on your abdomen.

Contemplate your navel. Each inhalation is twice as deep as you have been accustomed to. Now see the exhalation leaving your body through the navel, a misty stream of stress, going out. Count down from 50 to zero in rhythm with your focused breathing. When you reach ten, you will be fast asleep till morning.

Suggestion
"I sleep better all through the night, and stay alert all day, my body is energetic, and my personality has changed to cheerful from gloomy."

ITCHING...
You can stop the itch before you scratch. We know that scratching worsens an itchy condition and can lead to breaks in the skin, making it open to infection. You will learn to control sensory feelings and take command over the impulse. Whether an insect bite, poison ivy, Oak or Sumac or an allergic rash, scratching interferes with healing.

Imagery
Relief comes when you focus your thought far away from the area. Next, imagine the troublesome part being washed clean by a country waterfall. Feel the cool sensation rippling over your skin.

Suggestion
"Every time I think of a waterfall, that will be a signal to my brain to stop the itch, immediately. This is a post hypnotic suggestion."

JET LAG ADJUSTMENT...
People who travel by plane are familiar with the resulting daytime fatigue and nighttime insomnia that adds to the stress of travel. You don't have to put up with jet lag if you do self-hypnosis when you travel.

Imagery
See yourself seated in a plane with headphones or an audio tape player. You are programming your mind to reset your mental clocks. See yourself reset your watch to the time you plan to arrive at your new destination.

Suggestion

"I will adjust and cope with time changes without mental, physical or emotional disturbance."

JOB TRAINING...

Building skills to upgrade one's work status begins with the right attitude. Preparation for a career or job change takes self-mastery and confidence in one's abilities to take on challenges and grow with them. You will learn to live in the present and ignore past limitations.

Imagery

See yourself working at something you enjoy. You are smiling and thinking positive. A sign above your desk or work bench reads: ATTITUDE + ACTION = ACHIEVMENT.

Suggestion

"I am strongly motivated to improve my status. Every day, in every way, I become more and more skilled and successful. I have everything that it takes to move up the success ladder."

KLEPTOMANIA...

People who steal things that do not belong to them may be trying to call attention to their need for emotional support. Some psychoanalysts say the kleptomaniac is usually a women, trying to compensate for lack of a penis. Whether the petty thief is a man or a woman, whatever the cause, hypnosis offers the cure:

Imagery

Picture yourself in a tempting situation. You are surrounded by easy to steal objects, with no one around to interfere. However, in stead of giving in to the urge to steal, you stop, think it over, and make a mindful decision that stealing is inappropriate.

Suggestion

"I have overcome my weakness. I will never slip back to taking things that don't belong to me. Kleptomania is beneath me. I have too much self-respect to steal things that belong to other people."

LEARNING...

Learning begins with a sense of inner peace and freedom from fear of failure. Students find self-hypnosis makes study time more effective. It improves concentration and results in higher test scores. The power of your mind can bring you tenacious discipline to spur you on to your goals.

Imagery

Visualization takes on a special importance. When you enter the hypnotic alpha level, you open your eyes and focus on the test you need to learn. You have in-the-moment awareness and heightened receptivity.

Suggestion

"Learning has become so easy. My memory and recall are both keen and dependable under all conditions."

LUMBAGO...

Lower back pain, due to muscular strain, can become chronic. Some people resort to unnecessary surgery, when stress reduction may help. Using hypnosis, pain alleviation takes place after reaching the CORE stage. However, this can only happen when there is readiness to let go of the condition.

Imagery

After deep relaxation, focus is concentrated on the lower back. See the painful area as twice as large with an exit hole in the center. As you exhale ten, slow, consecutive breaths, imagine the pain going out with the air, right out of the exit hole.

Suggestion

"With every breath I breathe, the pain is diminishing. It is growing less and less. The pain is dissolving, melting away. Now, it is gone and will never return."

MALAISE...

A run-down, overall feeling of lethargy and weakness. When doctors find no organic cause, attitude may be the culprit. Malfunction of any one part of the body often reflects itself in every other area. Bad circulation, improper breathing, nervous tension, and poor digestion all contribute to malaise. Conversely, when all parts of the body are working in healthy harmony, they enthuse emotions and attitude.

Imagery

The movie screen is a perfect technique to use here. As the camera draws to a close-up of a group of famous healers. You recognize yourself as your own best healer. You are an energetic, healthy, happy person. What you see, can become your reality.

Suggestion

'I feel a surge of energy. I eat properly. I exercise. I have friends and family that love me. I have every reason to rejoice and become better and better, every day, in every way."

MALIGNANCY.

Researchers report there is an emotional profile which is a component to the disease. Hypnosis is not only a prevention method, it is also used to adjust to symptomatic discomfort and pain, as well as toleration of chemotherapy.

Imagery

Visualize yourself strolling in the country on a beautiful day in the summer. You are aware of all of your senses to enjoy each day of life. You see the colors of flowers. You smell the aroma. A breeze blows through your hair and it feels very pleasant. You hear your favorite music. Now you are singing and dancing, instead of worrying.

Suggestion

"The problem is going with every breath I breathe. I expect full recovery. I feel healthy and strong right now. Nothing and no one can upset me. Soon I will be back to my normal self."

MAKE MORE MONEY...

Financial success requires self-development and motivation. It is based on the formula: Attitude + Action = Achievement. Successful strategies begin in the mind. You have to Plan the Work and Work the Plan. Once you know what you want, be open to unexpected good news about finances.

Imagery

Imagine the phone ringing. When you answer, you are told you are about to receive a vast amount of money. See a truck delivering it to your front door. You shovel it up and fill your front room.

Suggestion

"I anticipate, look forward to good news. Everything that needs to be done will be done by me, to make the money come to me soon. I am prepared. If it is going to be, it is up to me to make it happen."

MASTURBATION OBSESSION...

Hypnosis methods to moderate the libido, and control one's physical reflexes have proven successful. In most cases. Where the problem is not linked to serious neurosis, such as fear and avoidance of normal intercourse with a mate.

Imagery

See yourself as a great lover. You have become skilled at pleasing your partner and you are appreciated. The interaction is so much more satisfying than the lonely act of masturbation.

Suggestion

"I will not limit myself to solo sex, but will reach out socially, and find more mature satisfaction. I enjoy pleasing another person as well as myself."

MARIJUANA CESSATION...

Hypnosis can recall the feeling without side affects. This works wonders for those users who are ready to change to a healthier high. Dr. Franz E. Winkler, in his booklet, *"About Marijuana,"* states, "An early effect of marijuana and hashish use is a progressive loss of will-power, noticeable to the trained observer after six weeks." An additional report is the study conducted by Dr. R. Campbell of Edmonton, Canada. Dr. Campbell, who works at Alberta's acute psychiatric ward, indicates that serious health problems can result. "There is a real danger that as little as one experience with marijuana could cause psychotic disorders, such as paranoia, withdrawal, depression, which could linger for months or even years after the drug experience."

Imagery

After progressive relaxation is accomplished, the split screen is employed. Here's how it works: On one side of the screen, picture yourself at your worst, a severely addicted, irresponsible, weak person. On the other side, what you can be when you quit the habit.

Suggestion

"I am ready to overcome my weakness and face life with strength and personal power. My breathing brings me increased energy and my mind and emotions are high."

MEMORY RECALL...

Your mental warehouse has vast accumulations of helpful information, but also a great backlog of useless debris. The sooner you give your mind a house cleaning, the better your memory will be. Hypnosis is the broom, which can sweep it clean. When bad experiences leave an after image, (like bad food leaves an aftertaste) hypnosis can erase the taste and replace the space with more satisfying visions.

Imagery

Visualize your memory warehouse as a computer. Everything has been recorded in your documents and files. All you have to do is push the right buttons to bring the information up on the monitor or screen. Form a mental image of the things you are trying to recall. Envision the situation in which the person or incident occurred. See the calendar with the day, month and year. Zero in on the wanted information.

Suggestion

"I will awaken each morning alert and aware. My mind will be sharp and clear all through the day and evening. As I fall asleep each night I will affirm that every day in every way my memory has become better and better."

MENAPAUSE...

Women passing through a period of hot flushes and anxiety about changing as they grow older, need a discipline to bolster their endocrine system and self-esteem. It helps to think young and act young and ignore the effects of passing time.

Imagery

The cool waterfall in the country on a calm summer day is a helpful vision. See yourself in a bikini, looking like a teenager. You see a lovely waterfall flowing into a shallow pool. Step into the pool and stand under the spray and feel yourself cool down.

Suggestion

"I feel calm and youthful; my glands are functioning appropriately. Any discomfort is temporary. I adjust easily to physical changes which are natural."

METABOLISM INCREASE...

There is, in your central brain, a small area which regulates the biochemistry of your body. Located in the hypothalamus, it controls both appetite and food storage in the form of excess fat. Medium to deep hypnosis can influence your subconscious to increase the burning up of stored fat by increasing the input of oxygen through deep breathing and diminishing the number of calories.

Imagery

Begin by seeing yourself in the relaxed posture. Your hand is resting on the abdomen and you feel fullness as you inhale. This calls for the mirror technique to see the results of increased metabolism. See the improved body changes. You are brimming over with energy. Your body's chemistry has changed and your metabolism is working at top speed.

Suggestion

"My metabolism is vigorous. Every time I enter this dimension of the mind, my metabolism will increase, bringing me the most energy with the least calories. My fat cells have been converted into boundless physical zest and emotional enthusiasm."

MOTION SICKNESS...

For some people traveling to get somewhere is no fun. Whether in a car, bus, train or plane, symptoms of motion sickness include paleness, sweating, upset stomach, dizziness and vomiting.

Imagery

Visualization and corrective suggestion brings the best results when you practice in advance of the trip. This is a problem that is solved with trance-rehearsal of the event. Using the mind-movie technique, see the screen. Picture the beginning of the trip, the middle, and the ending. All stages are pleasant.

Suggestion

"I will make the best of the situation. In a car, I sit in the front seat and do not look out the window. In an airplane, I sit over the wings. Aboard a ship, I stay toward the center and look way out into the horizon. In general, I don't read while moving, and avoid heavy food or alcohol before travel."

MOLESTATION/CHILD ABUSE...

Well over 400,000 reports of sexual assaults against children are filed with authorities every year by teachers and doctors who deal with traumatized kids. This supports the figures released by the Child Welfare League of America, which confirmed a 42 percent increase in reported complaints. Both victim and victimizer can be helped with hypnosis, if there is willingness to change.

Imagery

Regression is the technique of choice. Because it enables both the victim and abuser to better understand the underlying cause of the problem. Start with the blackboard and write: "Why did this happen?" When you get an answer, use the "Movie-of-the-Mind" to regress to the first incident that traumatized you.

Suggestion

"I understand the reason that this happened to me and it will never ever happen again."

MOOD SWINGS...

Chemical imbalance has been blamed for this problem. However, many people have normalized their emotional stability through mental persuasion. Try it before you overdose on medications that may have serious side effects. You will learn to listen to your mind's wisdom. To rationalize before you emotionalize. Self-hypnosis can be the turning point to lift your spirits from low to high, permanently.

Imagery

See yourself coming out of a state of lethargy with a rush of self-confidence and powerful energy. Use your Movie-of-the Mind" to spur a new kind of action.

Suggestion

"I have changed my attitude from negative to positive. I have filled with hope and live in the moment to celebrate the joy of life.

MOTIVATION...

Our degree of motivation depends on the reward. Hope can take over despair if you have a positive program for change. When motivation is fired by passionate desire, things happen quicker. The very fact that you are reading this book indicates that you are motivated to improve. Hypnosis can spur you to your goal. That is, if you practice with regularity.

Imagery

See your goals succeed; all of your desires actualized. This vision is best realized with the mind-movie technique. Remember to see a calendar with the projected date you have set for accomplishment.

Suggestion

"I have a burning desire to fulfill my life and enjoy all that I visualize for myself. I deserve it. I want it and I am motivated to get it as soon as possible. Each day, I check on what needs to be done, and I do it."

MOMISM...

Excessive attachment to one's mother which persists into adulthood, can keep the person from developing mature, intimate relationships. In extreme cases of mother-child attachment, the grown-up child may have problems of a sexual nature, because of unconscious, early guilt-associations.

Imagery
Regression to childhood will help the client discover what prompted the mother to raise a child who grows into adulthood with immature dependency. The purpose of regression is for the subject to gain awareness of cause and effect; and with that information be able to cut the apron strings.

Suggestion
"I am ready to get a life for myself, and will help my mother become aware that she can also be independent. I will radiate charisma to attract the right partner."

MUSIC AS THERAPY...
Meditation music played softly in the background, is extremely conducive to deepening the hypnotic trance. It should be low key without sudden changes. Baroch and other classical music tends to be in the alpha rhythm, which produces deep relaxation vibrations for stress reduction.

Imagery
Close your eye when listening to music whether you are at a concert or at home. Feel the music enter your mind and flow through the nerves of your body. Think of the pleasant sound as a therapeutic force and direct its energy to any part of your body that needs healing or strengthening.

Suggestion
"Every time I hear pleasant music it will soothe my emotions and my soul. My mind will automatically seek out any healing that needs to be done and the music will contribute to my wellness."

MUTILATION OF SELF...
There are people who pick acne blemishes until they bleed. Others scratch when there is no itch. Some even use knives to disfigure themselves. On the surface they simply seem stressed out, but on a deeper level, they lack sufficient self-worth, which is expressed in this destructive manner.

Imagery

Use the split screen. One side the ultimate destructive appearance. On the other side you see your best self looking free of all disfigurement.

Suggestion

"I am free of the obsolete behavior of self abuse.

It serves no positive purpose and gives a self-demeaning impression to others. I care about myself too much to hurt myself."

NAIL BITING...

This habit indicates to others that the person is overcome with anxiety. If a hypnotist is dealing with a child, background information from the parents needs to be examined. Chances are emotional problems need to be corrected, as well as the nail-biting. If the subject is an aware adult, nail biting can usually be stopped in one to two sessions with the following technique:

Imagery

Picture yourself at a professional manicurist, having your nails done. She has a bottle marked with an X for danger. One by one, she covers the tips of your finger-nails with this antidote. As you visual this press down the finger. Notice that the solution has a pungent smell that indicates a bitter taste. At this point, the client is told to focus on each finger nail, starting with the little finger on the right hand, and going to the little finger on the left hand.

Suggestion

"As I focus on each finger, I say to myself, 'this fingernail will never ever again be bitten by me. When people see nails that are abused, they get the wrong impression of my character. I am strong and free from the old tensions."

NARCOLEPSY...

This is a tendency to fall asleep during the day at inappropriate times. The Department of Transportation tells us 200,000 auto accidents are sleep related. A client came to me for help, after narrowly escaping a serious crash when he dozed off at the wheel. The following therapeutic techniques helped him a great deal. I should add, he was also on medication, and referred to me by his physician.

Imagery

Select the appropriate situation from the following: At the wheel driving; at the office working; at home with the family; or any other that suits you.

Suggestion

I will remain awake and alert except when I'm supposed to fall asleep. When I go to bed, I will sleep soundly and wake up rested and thoroughly refreshed, to remain awake and alert all through the day."

NECROPHILIA...

This sexual aberration deals with the desire to have sexual intercourse with a dead person. There is often a direct link to an event in childhood, such as losing a loving person that one did not have the opportunity to express their affection to. In adulthood, childhood trauma takes on sexual tones

Imagery

Regression to the childhood incident will bring with it awareness of the inappropriate acting out in adulthood.

Suggestion

"I am an adult with normal desires for fulfillment. Each and every time that I enter my hypnotic CORE, I will automatically wipe out the obsolete urges."

NIGHTMARES...

Grotesque images during sleep, such as killers threatening one's life, are expressions of unresolved fear, experienced during the waking hours. Occasional bad dreams are nothing to worry about. However, persistent repetitive ones, are trying to inform you of something you must do, in your own best interest. A helpful technique is to hypnotize yourself at bedtime, with suggestions to recall and understand the message behind the dream.

Imagery

As you prepare to fall asleep, use self-hypnosis to reach into your subconscious memory, to recall and examine the message in the disturbing dream.

Suggestion

"I will write down my dreams each morning when I wake up and the next night ask my subconscious mind to tell me what the message is for me."

NUMBNESS...

Lack of sensation can happen in any part of the body, but is most commonly found in hands and feet. Hypnotic focus can bring about sensitization through the use of visualization to increase normal circulation to the distressed area.

Imagery

After general relaxation, become aware of your breathing pattern. Slow down the rhythm and pinpoint the exhalation to the spot that need help. For example: Imagine the hands as the part you are working to improve. Picture a tiny opening at the tip of each finger; as the outgoing breath flows, it carries sensitivity to the fingertips. This increases circulation and nerve energy, eliminating numbness.

Suggestion

"With every breath I take, asleep or awake, I am normalizing my hands and fingers. The numbness is gone from every area and will not return."

OBSESSIVE-COMPULSIVE DISORDER (OCD)...

A typical example is that of the person who is driven to wash his/her hands excessively. Fear of contamination can take many form such as fear of sitting near someone who "didn't look clean." Another is avoiding cracks in the sidewalk, or fearing people of other races or religions. Repetitive, intrusive unwanted thoughts need to be replaced with positive suggestions and a visualization to reinforce desired results.

Imagery

You are seated in a movie theater, watching a film. The performer resembles you, with a similar problem. As you see it acted out you realize that it is illogical, inappropriate and foolish. You direct the ending and see the person behave in a normal way.

Suggestion

"I am changing for the better. When I first start to obsess, I take time to think it over before acting it out. After I think it over, it doesn't make sense, so my feelings change, and when my thoughts and feelings change, I stop obsessing and behave normally."

ORGANIZATION/NEATNESS...

We must all become organized, and prepared for life's opportunities. The time is now to get rid of any obsolete obstacles to your success. Eliminate the clutter from your surrounding, as well as any cluttered, confused thinking patterns.

Imagery

See your home environment. There is a place for everything; and everything is in it's place. Imagine a "neatness inspector" going through your place. See him point out what needs to be done to get your life in order. Go from room to room and clean up.

Suggestion

"I will straighten up my home and straighten up my life. Obstacles are merely challenges to my intelligence. I want to clear the path to success".

ORGAN TRANSPLANTS...

One can lessen the danger of rejection by hypnosis, and awake positive auto-suggestion. To cut the risk of negative side effects preparation of the patient before he/she undergoes surgery helps in avoiding problems. Later this is reinforced with the following method.

Imagery

It helps to first look at a chart, showing the healthy anatomy of the organ that has been transplanted. After reaching deep trance level, see the chart once again in your mind's eye. Study the function of the organ and accept it as your own.

Suggestion

"The organ is now mine. I love it and intend to keep it functioning well in my long, strong life without problems."

ORGASM RELEASE...

There is nothing more effective than orgasm for totally relaxing the nervous system. Unfortunately, many people (more females than males) are too up-tight to allow this climactic feeling to take over.

Imagery

See yourself in bed with the world's greatest lover who is devoted to pleasing you. Think of the strongest, longest lasting orgasm you ever had, then say to yourself:

Suggestion

"I feel the sensation growing stronger and stronger. I am ready. It is happening. NOW! WOW!" (Afterward, give suggestion for the future). I am sexually normal and have everything it takes to feel genital sensation increase to the point of orgasm. Every time I have sex, it turns out to be better and better."

PAIN ALLEVIATION...

Researchers have known for a long time that the brain is the source of pain perception. Now we also know the brain manufactures a morphine-like pain-killer which is stimulated by the hypnotic state of mind. The marvel of this fact is that you can get the same results naturally without becoming addicted. Pain responds to mental imagery and suggestion on a regional basis.

Imagery

Using focused breathing, imaging a small hole in the area of pain and exhale the pain with the outgoing breath. Breathe in fully and exhale forcefully. Next see yourself completely free of pain. You are actively engaged in exercises or sport activity that you did before the problem.

Suggestion

"Each time I picture the healing light directed into the troubled area. I see it melt in the warm rays; it is shrinking into a tiny size, disappearing now."

PALPITATIONS...

Any concern about one's heart, should be checked with physician. When the condition is the result of stress, hypnosis is a safe, drug-free antidote, and can be supportive of medical treatment.

Imagery

When you reach a deep CORE trance, you are aware of your breathing. You place your right hand on the left side of your chest and feel the inhalations and exhalations. You are smiling. You are free from anxiety. Next, suggestions are directed to the heart.

Suggestion

"Dear heart, you are healthy and happy; normal and calm. Your rhythm is perfectly balanced with nature."

PANIC ATTACKS...

Over 50 million people in the USA suffer from panic attacks, and the number is increasing as pressures escalates. Nausea, sweating, dizziness, pains in chest, shortness of breath are all symptoms which respond to hypnosis. For those with an extreme problem it might include fear of dying, going crazy or losing control of bodily functions or if driving, losing control and having an accident.

Imagery

Picture a "Movie-of-the-Mind." See yourself in a stressful predicament, but instead of reacting with panic you are cool, confident, and concentrated on yourself as an empowered person. Because anxiety shortens the breath, deliberately breathe deeply and slowly, focusing on the exhalation. As you expel the air, think of it as expelling the discomfort.

Suggestion

"I will stop limiting my life. I will exchange panic for enlightenment, and stop thwarting myself. Movement through life becomes simpler when it is based on the unifying principle of a balanced cohesive being."

PEDIPHILIA...

The sexual exploitation of children by emotionally disturbed people (mostly men) has become epidemic. Some are arrested. However, the recidivism rate for untreated perpetrators is about fifty percent. Behavioral therapy with applied hypnosis can reduce this percentage considerably, depending on individual motivation and intelligence. Hypnosis not only can change the behavior of the pediphile, but is also valuable to erase the painful memories from the minds of the child victims.

Imagery

Both victim and victimizer need help from a trained psychologist who uses hypnosis. Abreaction is accomplished by hypnotic regression to the original root of the problem.

Suggestion

For the victim: "I am free of the scars that have pained me. I am ready to get on with my life."

For the pediphile: "I will never ever sexually molest a child again. I will behave in a mature way."

PEPTIC ULCERS...

Symptoms of peptic ulcers vary depending on where the ulcer is located. Duodenal ulcers may cause burning, gnawing or an aching sensation. Gastric ulcers, located in the stomach may be accompanied by nausea and vomiting. In either case, pain may follow after a meal. Hypnosis can not only alleviate the symptoms but can lessen the cause, which is usually stress related.

Imagery

Internalize your visualization. Imagine that you have a searchlight and you are exploring the internal organs of your digestive system. Because ulcers are caused by a tiny organism that lives in the mucous gel that lines the wall of your stomach, shine the dissolving light into the bacteria and wipe it out. See the ulcer diminishing and disappearing.

Suggestion

"I will remain centered and relaxed under all situations. If there is a conflict, I will be assertive as well as cooperative."

PERMISSIVE TECHNIQUE...

In contrast to authoritative, stage-hypnosis, the permissive hypnotist uses a gentle approach with client-approval to assure cooperation: "You will enjoy a pleasant experience by drifting into a soothing state of serenity. Begin by focusing your eyes up toward the ceiling. That's good. Now breath slowly and deeply. That's right. Place your hand on your diaphragm and feel the rhythm of your breathing. Take five deep breaths as I count backward from five to zero. When you hear zero that is a signal to close your eyes. That's right. You're doing just fine."

Imagery

Next, picture every part of your body relaxing, starting at the top of your head and working down to the tips of your toes. As I mention a part of your body, see that part of you and letting go.

Suggestion

Hypnotist; "Every time you hear my voice, and I say 'Go deeper' that is a signal for you to let yourself drift into a state of serenity and peace of mind."

*When practicing the techniques, remember that your emotional tone of voice is crucial to success. It should be low key without sudden changes. Meditation music played softly in the background is also conducive to deepening the cooperation.

PHANTOM LEG OR ARM...

Amputees tend to suffer pain in the absent limb because the reflex system has not registered the loss. Hypnosis, conducted by a medical hypnotist, can direct the brain to contact the body and relay the message to stop the pain.

Imagery

See your body with realistic awareness that there is no reason to feel pain. The pain has evaporated. See your very capable doctors preparing to assist you in rehabilitation to make the best of your condition.

Suggestion

"The pain is gone and will not return. I will heal rapidly and be prepared as soon as possible for successful reparation and adjustment to my condition."

PHOBIAS...

An irrational anxiety and/or panic that has no basis in reality. The obsessive dread can be of anything because it is based on an unreal beliefs. The law of belief says whatever we believe becomes our reality. Beliefs form a telescope through which we view our individual worlds. Phobias are the distorted telescopes which need to be repaired or discarded.

Imagery

You are in a movie theater, watching a film about someone with your particular phobia. The performer bears a striking resemblance to yourself. Notice how irrational the behavior seems to you. Now you are the director — Change the scene as you know an intelligent person should behave in a such a situation.

Suggestion

"The phobia is losing it's hold on me. When the foolish fear begins to annoy me, instead of giving in, I will assert my power and take positive action that is useful for my well-being."

PHOTOGRAPHY...

Hypnosis is valuable to improve the photographer's concentration and focus. Also, it is helpful for communicating with the model, or celebrity subject, to receive the best, cooperative response.

Imagery

A light self-hypnosis is all that is needed here. The photographer, pauses for a moment, rolls his eyes upward and then opens them with a vision of what he wants in this photo.

Suggestion

"I know what I want in this photo and I know how to get it." To model, he/she sets the mood: "Think of yourself at the beach on a beautiful summer day. Hear the waves rolling on to the shore, etc."

PHOTOMANIA...

At its extreme, this represents an abnormal compulsion to be in the spotlight, even at inappropriate times. A more common example is the person who fears the dark, and can only sleep with a light on. The obsession, harks back to childhood

Imagery

To erase the reflexive reaction, we must regress to the origin of the phobia. This must be done with the skill of a professional therapist. When the subject recalls an important incident, a finger signal is given to the hypnotist, who provides pad and pen for the subject to write out his/her remembrances. The trauma is then wiped out by several techniques, such as the waterfall, or spiritual light.

Suggestion

The therapists should record an audio tape for the client as follows: "You are now free from fear and anxiety. Any time in the future, if you are in a situation that once troubled you, say to yourself: 'I have overcome. I am strong. I am normal in every way. The problem is gone and will not return.' This post hypnotic suggestion will work at all times."

PICA...

This is obsessive craving for certain foods, often occurs during pregnancy, but can also be a problem for anyone. This is especially important for those with high cholesterol, blood pressure, diabetes and other physical ailments where certain types of food may be harmful.

Imagery

See a table laden with all kinds of food. Picture yourself selecting exactly what is right for your condition. Take a garbage bag and dump the rest into it. For you, bad food is garbage,

Suggestion

"My urges for bad food has diminished. I am self-empowerment. I know what's right and I will do it."

PIERCING...

Whether it's for ear lobes, nose holes, eyebrows, tongue, or belly button, knowledgeable people know it can be done painlessly, when hypnosis is used. Some people see a hypnotist in advance to learn self-hypnosis to help adjust to the change.

Imagery

Before deciding to have the procedure done, hypnosis should be used to visualize how this change in appearance will affect your life. In a light to medium trance, see the magic-mind mirror. Use the split screen technique. On one side, see your normal self; on the other, picture yourself after the piercing. Ask yourself whether this will enhance or detract from job opportunities, relationships, etc.

Suggestion

"I have made the right decision. I am comfortable with myself. I like the way I look and feel satisfied with my self-image."

PILES/HEMORHOIDS

This requires medical references. Uncomfortable itching and swelling can be controlled and even eliminated with diligent practice of affirmative imagery and self-programming.

Imagery

To reinforce convention treatment, picture yourself as a proctologist, give yourself an examination. As you examine the rectal orifice, see yourself shining a white light into the troublesome part of your body.

Suggestion

"Every time I visualize a white light shining into my rectum, I will encourage the healing process."

POISON IVY...

Allergic reaction to plants can be avoided or lessened by conditioning with hypnotic suggestion, even before the actual symptoms appear.

Imagery

See yourself walking on a path in the country on a lovely day. You are alert and aware when you see poison ivy or any other plant that affects you. If you are not sure about a plant, you don't take risks.

Suggestion

"I will be able to recognize the plant and by so doing avoid contact. In addition, I am building a strong resistance to its affect. My natural defenses are growing stronger and stronger. If I get the problem in spite of my care, I will not scratch or aggravate the lesions. Instead I will send healing images."

POLICE WORK...

Many police departments throughout the country, employ hypnotists as an aid to interrogation. While not accepted in many cases as legal evidence, it is very valuable as corroborative information and often uncovers hidden facts, which solve cases.

Imagery

The police hypnotist uses regression to the time of the incident. This will help the witness remember details. Automatic writing is very useful, here, as it can be shown later for evidence.

Suggestion

Hypnotist: "Picture, imagine, visualize the incident, and write out all that you see, hear, and feel that may be of importance, to the solving of this case."

POLITICIANS...

Many candidates running for office, 'Psych-up' for added confidence, especially before delivering a major speech, or facing a new challenge.

Imagery

Picture yourself making a speech in front of a group of enthusiastic supporters. Every thing you say is met with cheers. Banners and pictures are waved by the participants in the audience.

Suggestion

"I have everything it takes to be a winner. I am motivated, educated, and prepared to take office."

POST HYPNOTIC SUGGESTION...

For improvement after a professional session to be long lasting, the subject is given a long term suggestion to reinforce the programming after he/she leaves. A triggering action is set up. For example: "Each time you drink a glass of juice, you will feel satisfied without alcohol."

Imagery

You see yourself at a party with friends who are offering you what you shouldn't have (drinks, drugs, fatty foods...etc.) You let them know that you are now free of the bad habit. This image will carry over into the waking state with post-hypnotic suggestions.

Suggestion

Post hypnotic suggestion works, without anyone being aware that we are being programmed. "Each time I trigger my post-hypnotic suggestion, I activate the force which flashes the message to me when I need it."

POSTURE...

The mind directs the body which expresses your sense of esteem and worthiness. Posture is part of the demeanor that we radiate to others. This conveys the level of our self-esteem.

Imagery

See yourself standing in front of a three-panel mirror. Your shoulders are back. Your head is held high. You look like a winner. Your body is in perfect balance; mind and emotions are in harmony.

Suggestion

"I am projecting my best self-image. People treat me with high-regard because I look like I deserve it."

PREGNANCY COMFORT...

Women don't have to suffer the side effects of being pregnant. Nausea, restless sleep, sticking to a healthy diet, fear of the birth experience, the need to stop smoking, eliminate drugs, and any other bad habits. From the moment of conception until delivery, the expectant mother should practice self-hypnosis for health and a painless delivery. As in any endeavor, you must apply yourself to learning the method described here, for you.

Imagery
See the unborn infant floating in its secure lake of tranquillity, within the warmth of your body. This indwelling security is both physical and emotional. The fetus is affected by your movements and emotions, both negative and positive. Communicate your love.

Suggestion
"I will stick to a healthy lifestyle and maintain serene, happy emotions. My birthing will be easy and pain free. As soon as I feel the first contraction, I will enter bliss consciousness, and repeat to myself: 'I am a healthy, normal and my baby will slip out easily.' I am ready to be a great mother."

PRE-MENSTRUAL SYNDROME (PMS)...
For many women this represents irritability, and mood swings. Emotions may seem to be riding a roller-coaster. All that ceases, when you prepare yourself a week in advance of your period, with positive expectations by using hypnosis and positive self-talk.

Imagery
Picture the calendar at that certain time of the month. See yourself smiling. Hear yourself laughing. Picture yourself standing in front of the mirror of your mind and looking at your body with pride and satisfaction. Tummy flat. No bloating.

Suggestion
"I have overcome the problem and it will never ever return. I look forward to healthy, happy days every single day of the month."

PRISONS...
Society must seize the opportunity that forced enclosure presents, to turn inmates around so they stop being criminals. Teaching them self-hypnosis will help them develop confidence and work skills to get back into the mainstream

and be self-supporting. A list is provided to each person to choose the program wanted. They also are given aptitude tests, which helps determine the most successful kind of work for them to pursue.

Imagery

After the hypnotic level is reached, remote viewing techniques are used as follows: The subject conceives him/herself as being in the audience watching a film about "someone's life." The subject recognizes as his/herself on a pleasant job and doing very well.

Suggestion

"I gained great insight from this experience. It has matured me and brought enlightenment to improve myself. I have the intelligence and self-esteem to overcome problems. I am changing for the better."

PSORIASIS...

This manifests itself as scaly, red irritated patches usually attack elbows, scalp, and eyebrow and to a lesser degree, other areas of the body. Hypnosis has been known to prevent flare-ups and diminish the severity. However, The sooner the skin disturbance is recognized the better hypnotic suggestion works.

Imagery

As you focus into the most severe part of your skin, you see that the condition is diminishing. As you keep concentrating into the spot, it disappears.

Suggestion

"I expect; I anticipate; and insist that the condition correct itself with the power of my determination and regular practice of hypnosis."

PSYCHOSOMATIC ILLNESS...

Physical dysfunction, when non-organic, is referred to as "psychosomatic." This term indicates the effect of the mind (psyche) on the body soma). Emotions, inhibited instead of expressed can cause physical symptoms, such as: headaches, backaches, ulcers, skin rashes and a host of other tension related emotions. Hypnosis converts negative emotions to positive ones.

Imagery

Keep in mind that the deleterious effects of stress and negative emotions will manifest through the weakest and most vulnerable part of your body. Focus into that spot and see and feel radiant healing.

Suggestion

"I am aware that bad thoughts can make you sick, and good thoughts can make you well. I choose to stay well and my mind will make sure I prevent illness.

PSYCHE-YOURSELF UP...

The ability to perform unusual physical feats is an art that anyone is capable of with brain-training such as hypnosis. It only takes an alpha or hypnoidal level. We can see this in the sports arena, where gold medal winners "psyche" themselves up to surpass their own records.

Imagery

Visualize yourself in a challenging situation. You are calm. You are cool. You are confident. Now you are performing the act with the greatest skill that is possible. You receive a winner's prize and lots of congratulations from all the onlookers.

Suggestion

"My mind is sharp and clear. My body is alert and balanced. They are interacting with each other to optimize my success. I become better and better."

PUBLIC SPEAKING...

Whether it's a complex prepared presentation, or just among friends, you can project thoughts with expertise if you rehearse the speech while in a light trance. Whether you need the skill in politics, business, or social interaction, what you say and how you say it, can open doors or have them shut in your face.

Imagery

You are at a meeting, standing at the lectern, facing the group, and making eye contact. You are prepared, with a strong opening sentence. You also have rehearsed the body of your speech, and aware of the conclusion. See a capsule performance of your address and hear the applause.

Suggestion

"It will be easy for me to speak before an audience because I will be prepared, by rehearsing in advance. I am confident and will project my voice, clearly. I am informative, entertaining and persuassive."

PYROMANIA...

This is an uncontrollable desire to be around fire. When unchecked may lead to arson and death not only of innocent victims but of the perpetrator as well. There is a root to this disorder. The original trauma can be wiped out with hypnosis.

Imagery

This requires the assistance of a skilled hypno-therapist, schooled in psychology. The subject is regressed to a time in childhood when an incident occurred involving fire. At this point, the subject is given pad and pen to answer a list of questions which have been agreed upon before induction.

Suggestion

Prearranged suggestions are similar to these: "When the urge to start a fire occurs to me, I will stop in my tracks and reconsider. I do not want to harm people. Fire causes pain and death and I am a decent person and don't want to harm innocent people."

QUALITY OF LIFE...

We can all reach up to a quality of living that surpasses what we now have. First it is necessary to see in the mind's eye, what would improve the quality of your life. Money? Love? Career?

Imagery

Visualize an abundant life with everything you have dreamed of. You have prospered and achieved your highest goals. See what a great life it could be if you reached your potential. See the kind of people you enjoy, surrounding you. What you see, you can be.

Suggestion

"I will do whatever is necessary to achieve prosperity to enhance the quality of my life. I have the motivation and the intelligence to reach upward."

QUARRELSOME...

This describes a person who habitually disagrees, is argumentative, and looking for conflict. Such an individual needs to be reprogrammed to present a more conciliatory attitude in communicating with other people. Awareness and willingness to change, are the first prerequisites.

Imagery

See yourself having an amiable discussion with a person who previously annoyed you. Although you do not see any merit to what that person is saying, you picture yourself as patiently waiting to express your differences in a calm manner.

Suggestion

"I am learning how to disagree without being disagreeable. I will listen to another point of view and be more flexible. I will compromise instead of being confrontational."

RAPE RECOVERY...

Every six minutes a woman is forcibly raped in the United States. That's about ten times higher than most European countries. Both victims and victimizers need help to understand the underlying motive and the prevention of future repetitions. Spiritual visualization works for both. Violent acts like rape, and child molestation leave their marks of fear and anger that require deep level hypnosis.

Imagery

See yourself walking up the side of a hill to a golden temple of purification — body, mind and soul. You enter and walk to the center to stand in golden beams of light which cascade down from a large crystal dome in the ceiling. Feel the rays of light enter the top of your head and flow through every cell of your body.

Suggestion

Repeat to yourself mentally: "The violence will never ever happen again. I have risen above the terrible experience and am free of emotional and physical pain. I am no longer angry and am a better person, now."

REBIRTHING...

This is a transformational experience, where you can release childhood anger and choose new emotional responses to family members, who may have interfered with your development. The experience revitalizes the over stressed body and refreshes the mind, returning one's original magnetic energy.

Imagery

Imagine floating in a lake of warm water Think of your feet as very light and airy, like balloons. Think of your toes as bubbles. Think of your ankles as loose, limp and disjointed, just dangling. Let your mind wander upward to your calf muscles. Think of your calf muscles as very heavy. Think of your knees as loose, limp, and disjointed; your thigh muscles as very heavy. Think of your hips as loose, limp, and disjointed. Think of your buttock muscles as very heavy. You are now relaxed from the tip of your toes up to the center of your body. Now start at your head and work down to the center.

Suggestion

"This magnetic fluid is rebirthing every cell of my body, every organ inside and outside, I'm nourished by the amniotic fluids of the earth's womb, which encourages new cells, and repairs those that need it."

REGRESSION...

It is empowering to examine, while in a trance state, events and emotions connected to the past. Prior happenings are viewed as steps to higher consciousness. You can transcend time and space and see things from a transcended place. "Oh strange, that in our embers, is something that remembers!"

Imagery

See yourself standing in front of a blackboard. Visualize a large white circle on the blackboard. See yourself in the center of the circle. Now the circle turns into a tunnel. You find yourself on a moving sidewalk, passing through the tunnel toward an open light that is very beautiful. When you reach the light you will be in another lifetime, as far back as you choose. See the color of your skin. Are you a man or a woman, adult or child? What do they call you? What part of the world is this? Hear the language being spoken; attend a ritual ceremony; taste the food; smell the aromas; listen to the music.

Suggestion

"I will gain great insight from this experience. It will bring me enlightenment to improve myself in this lifetime. Each time I choose to go into this space, I will get more information to help actualize myself."

RELATIONSHIP PROBLEMS...

We all need to be intimate with another person, but for many people there is an anticipation of failure, based on past situations. Hypnosis boosts confidence in social situations to make new friends that can turn into lovers. Your reward may very well be an everlasting relationship with the lover of your dreams.

Imagery

See yourself at a social gathering. You confidently make eye contact with an interesting person and project a caring personality. If you feel affection in your heart, it will be known to others by the look on your face, your posture, your demeanor.

Suggestion

"I am ready to correct my shortcomings, I am prepared to embark on a program of self-improvement. I can and I will fulfill my needs, attract and enjoy intimacy."

RELIGIOUS EVANGELISM...

Evangelists use authoritative hypnotic methods, similar to stage hypnotists to mesmerize their followers on television, while more mainstream theologians practice gentle, permissive, indirect hypnosis. The malleable brain finds itself invaded by a superior force and becomes obedient.

Imagery

Here's how it works: See yourself seated in the audience at a religious meeting. The evangelist invites you on to the stage, and asks you to state your problem. He evokes the power of a spiritual force to heal you. Believing in his superior power is crucial to the healing. Scientifically, we know that the subject's mind-power will actually do the healing.

Suggestion

"Look into my eyes and when I raise my hand up to your forehead your eyes will roll up and lids will close. When I tap your forehead, you will fall back and my assistant will catch you (it happens). The power of God has entered you. You are healed."

ROAD RAGE...

We are hearing reports of the sharp increase in fights on highways where guns come into play and death or injury results. The drivers must accept that a car can be a dangerous weapon in of itself and avid conflict.

Imagery

See yourself driving on a highway with an annoying driver trying to cut you off. Make the imagery as provoking as possible, but see yourself keeping your cool. The one who controls anger is the winner.

Suggestion

"This isn't worth getting hurt over. I will do everything to avoid confrontation. If I am forced into it I will negotiate instead of losing control."

ROCKING OBSESSION...

This is usually a link to childhood insecurity. Regression to the origin cause, can correct the reflex, whether the subject manifest it while seated or lying in bed. Induce the trance level then go into this visualization:

Imagery

Walking in the country, you see two trees. Hung between the trees, is a hammock. You look down into the hammock and see yourself as a small child. As you watch the child in the hammock, you see an adult developing. Now, you stop rocking in the hammock, and instead see yourself get up and walk tall. Each night, before bedtime, you will repeat the following:

Suggestion
"I am not a baby any more. I am filled with pride and satisfaction at my maturity. The rocking is gone."

ROSACEA...

This is a chronic facial, skin disorder, manifested by broken blood vessels causing redness and sometime swelling of the nose. The condition can be aggravated by anxiety, alcohol, and spicy foods.

Imagery
Picture yourself reflected in a mirror that enlarges your face so that the tiny blood vessels and red areas can be easily scrutinized. Especially focus on your nose and the surrounding area of skin. Next, place your finger tips gently on the affected area, and picture yourself stroking away the redness and the enlarged vessels. Finally see your reflection smiling back at you with skin that is clear and unblemished. While doing so, give yourself the following commands:

Suggestion
"I will avoid foods that aggravate my condition. Alcohol is out of bounds, as are other inappropriate substances that trigger the problem."

RESTLESS LEG SYNDROME...

Chronic jerking of the limbs interferes with getting a good night's sleep. Some sufferers complain of tingling, as well as creepy, crawly sensations. Compulsive, jump-out-of-bed reaction cause some people to get up during the night to walk the sensation off. This doesn't always work, and often results in habitual sleep deprivation.

Imagery
This visualization works best when you lie down in your bed and are ready to fall asleep. After the induction by relaxation, concentrate on your feet. Imagine your feet soaking in a large tub of warm water to which has been added a special herbal extract which eliminates the problem.

Suggestion

"I feel the magical fluid rising from the soles of my feet into my ankles, my calf muscles, the backs of my knees and into my thighs, hips and buttocks. All my muscles and nerves are coated with this creaming, healing, soothing feeling. My legs are so relaxed."

SADO-MASOCHISM...

Some people believe they can only function sexually at this level and do not seek out alternative ways of loving. For them, This is often a retaliation to the abuse in childhood. There is a tendency among humans to relive trauma from the past. Because of this early imprint on self-image, we need to take an inward journey to the original insult.

Imagery

Abreaction through hypnotic regression brings the problem into focus, allowing the eradication of its influence, if there is sufficient motivation to change. Visualize lovemaking that is all pleasure without pain. See the passion as a spiritual gift.

Suggestion

"I no longer need to feel pain to reach heights of sexual pleasure. I've had too much cruelty in my life and will not add to it, any longer."

SELF-ESTEEM...

Lack of self-esteem is the most common obstacle to happiness. Esteem is essential for success in all areas, such as relationships, job career, and mental/emotional health. You are the architect of your life — how strong or weak you appear to others, is based on the person, projected by you.

Imagery

With hypnosis, you are the artist of your own fine portrait. You decide how you wish others to see you. Visualize your portrait, as you would see a person of great importance, one who has achieved respect and acknowledgment, based on enhanced values.

Suggestion

"I will set an example for the way others treat me, by treating myself with great respect. I will never ever diminish myself in conversations with others."

SELF-HYPNOSIS...

Every person can enter a higher realm of energy, and train every cell of the body to respond to positive self-suggestion. Getting into the habit of directing the events in your life as well as your health, becomes easy with practice. These are the steps you can take any time you have the need:

STEP 1...

Find a secluded place where you will not be disturbed for twenty to thirty minutes. Recline in a comfortable position.

STEP 2...

Focus on breathing slower and deeper. Place your hand on your diaphragm and feel the difference. Count to four with inhale, six as you exhale.

STEP 3...

Pick a spot on the ceiling and focus your eyes. When the eyelids begin to feel heavy or blink, let them close.

STEP 4...

Now you will focus on your toes and then progressively relax your entire body, part by part. Feel your knees loosening, your thighs, hips, etc.

Imagery

Deepen the relaxation by picturing yourself standing at the top of a staircase holding a sturdy banister. As you descend, you count down from fifty to zero. Step by step, you go deeper and deeper into a calm state of suggestibility.

Suggestion

"Each time I relax deeply, I can enter the trance state. I will be able to return to the feeling whenever I choose." Affirmations and suggestion can be practiced effectively, no matter where we happen to be. This technique brings together mind and body, as you tap your wishes into your automatic motor system.

SEXUAL ADDICTION...

Those who obsess with sex are hooked in the same way as drug addicts. They calm themselves by indulging in instant gratification, seeking to alleviate helplessness and worthlessness. For this kind of addict, sex becomes a way of avoiding meaningful relationships. The partner, objectivized, is used as a means of personal satisfaction rather than a shared experience.

Imagery

See yourself in a relaxed, loving embrace. You are with a partner that shares some of your own interests in life. You are communicating on all levels. When the sex happens, you are equally interested in the pleasure of your mate, as you are for yourself.

Suggestion

"I will develop my sensuality and share mind, body and soul with the right person. I will attract the best partner by giving out the right vibrations."

SEXUAL DYSFUNCTION...

The following are the most common problems that respond to hypnotic suggestion:

· Low desire for sexual intercourse
· Erection difficulty, mental in origin
· Retarded orgasm due to stress factor
· Pain during penetration and thrusting
· Personality/relationship disagreements
· Matching a partner's frequency of desire

Imagery

Concentrate on your specific problem and when you enter the trance, see yourself as having conquered the problem. Once your mind has been fed these image builders, the feedback will help overcome fear of failure. Keep in mind that the most dominant thought focused upon is the one that is apt to be realized.

Suggestion

The most helpful thing to say to yourself before sexual intercourse, is, "Yes, I can get better and better!" and the most helpful thing you can say when it's over is, "And next time it will be even better."

SINGING...

Voice clarity improves, as well as tone and pitch, due to the absence of tension after a self-hypnosis session. A light to medium level is sufficient. Self-hypnosis is especially useful before a recording session and/or stage performances.

Imagery

You are placing a video tape into your VCR. Next, see yourself looking and sounding great. Lean back, smile, and enjoy your best performance.

Suggestion

"I am improving every day. I will stick to a practice and rehearsal routine. Practice makes perfect and I will reach my highest talent by working at success."

SKIN DISTURBANCES...

Whether an allergy, dermatitis, acne, or any of a number of skin disorders, imagery and positive suggestion can hasten the healing. Religious stigmata, (the reproduction of Christ's wounds is an example of how the mind can change the flesh of the body. A distinction is made by the church between scars caused by mental visualization alone, and those spiritually imposed. Theologians do not ignore that the power of the mind may be involved.

Imagery

Use the split-screen or mirror for the most dramatic visualization. See "Before and After Photos," and then cancel out the negative photo and enlarge the positive one, so that it covers the entire area.

Suggestion

See a commercial ad, featuring this banner slogan: The condition is now cured, and will not come back. Read the commercial out loud, five times, counting off on your fingers, while you go deeper into the trance.

SLEEPWALKING...

Sleepwalking is called "somnambulism' and is akin to hypnosis, because part of the brain is asleep and part is awake. This affects 10 to thirty percent of all Americans and usually begins before the age of 12. It can be dangerous as the afflicted person can walk out of the home and wander about without conscious awareness.

Imagery

After induction to a deep level, see yourself fast asleep in your bed, smiling contentedly. Then see a clock; Fast forward the time until morning. There is a sign over your bed "STAY IN BED UNTIL MORNING."

Suggestion

Say to yourself when you are ready to fall asleep each night: "I will remain safely in my bed until morning, and awaken feeling rested and refreshed."

SLEEP APNEA...

Usually accompanies deep snoring and irregular breathing patterns. This can lead to the cessation of breathing, where the victim awakens with a start, and then goes back to sleep, or in more severe cases, affect the normal heart beat.

Imagery

Picture yourself fast asleep. Self-hypnosis is called for here, and the exercise should be done at night just before nodding off into slumber. An audio tape is also useful, for those who resist self-induction.

Suggestion

"I am training my subconscious mind to signal me. At the first sign of the problem, I will shift my body to a side position, take a deep breath and continue in sleep until morning, when I will wake up full of pep."

SMOKING...

Millions of Americans are addicted to nicotine. One million teenagers start smoking every year. One third of them will die prematurely. If you don't want to be part of that sick statistic, here's an aversion visualization that has worked for millions who have quit the filthy habit, permanently.

Imagery

See yourself strolling in the country; the sun is shining and all is right with the world. You look up into a tree and see a bird, singing a melody. It's round chest is puffed out, as it breathes the clean air. You are aware of the air that you share with all life on this planet. Just as you would not blow smoke into the face of a bird, a kitten, or a child, so you do not blow smoke into your tender body. You are a valuable human being and have self-respect.

Suggestion

"With each breath, I am contented and satisfied without smoke. Other smokers will have no influence or tempt me to weaken. Each time the thought of a cigarette occurs to me, instead of lighting up, I will raise my arms overhead and take a deep breath."

SNORING...

This is usually due to blockage of nasal passages, combined with the vibration of the uvula and soft palate. Mouth breathing which triggers snoring usually occurs when one sleeps on one's back. Therefore, it helps the person who wishes to stop snoring to visualize sleeping in the side position.

Imagery

See yourself in your bed, sleeping in the side position. You look completely relaxed and serene. Your breathing is normal. there is no snoring. Say to yourself silently what I suggest out loud. You will repeat your suggestions just before you fall asleep:

Suggestion

"Any time I roll over on my back, this will remind me to change to the side position, and to breath smoothly from the diaphragm. I do not snore any more."

SOCIAL ANXIETY DISORDER...

This is fear-based shyness and avoidance of situations where we might be rejected or criticized. Sufferers may have panic reactions such as sweating, blushing, and find it difficult to have easy conversations, with new people.

Imagery
See yourself at a large social reception for an important person. People are all gathered around you because you are that important person.

Suggestion
"I am socially at ease. I will cease my old anxiety because it is contrary to my best interests. I am pleasant. People like me and I like them."

SOCIAL SKILLS...
People who grow up with inadequate role models at home, don't know how to behave in social situations. Hypnosis provides rapid training to prepare young people and others to show self-confidence, respect and interest in others.

Imagery
Let your mind drift to a party situation. You approach an attractive person and introduce yourself. Look that person in the eyes, smile with confidence. Engage the person into conversation by asking friendly questions about their work, culture preferences, etc.

Suggestion
"Each time I meet someone I am interested in knowing better, my confidence and social skills will improve."

SPACE TRAVEL...
Hypnosis can be part of the advance preparation to sail to the stars. It is a useful tool to help humans function more efficiently while moving through space. Hypnotic relaxation and trance induction can be utilized to reduce the metabolic rate and oxygen consumption. The digestive process will require less calories, reducing quantity of supplies.

Imagery
The hypnosis trance is used for preparation and rehearsal of procedures. Flexibility, living in tight quarters, the tolerance of weightlessness — are all experienced in advance of the trip.

Suggestion

"I am prepared, and enthused about interplanetary travel. I will be alert and aware of my surroundings and participate on any level required of me."

SPIRITUAL ENHANCEMENT...

Hypnosis heightens one's sensibility, to uncover the deeper mystery of life. Within the hypnotic womb of wellness, you become inner directed and spiritually protected against harm. Reaching your highest self, allows you to sponge out trauma, toxins and tension, to make a fresh start in life. The outer layers of perceptions, pretensions and environmental conditioning are easily assessed from a higher plane. Everything that you have warehoused is examined under a new radiant light.

Imagery

You are strolling in the country. You feel high-spirited and light footed as you move up a sloping hillside. Now you see an ancient temple, its golden dome shining in the sunlight. The door is open and there is a welcome mat, with your name on it. You enter the center where you are showered with golden light streaming down from a crystal ceiling dome.

Suggestion

"I feel the power enter me with its golden stream of light. This will bring me great insight, intuition and wisdom to become more spiritual."

SPORTS ABILITY...

The ability to perform unusual physical feats is an art that amazes outsiders. We can see why hypnosis is frequently practiced in the sports arena. Here gold medal winners "psyche themselves up" to surpass the records of others, as well as their own.

Imagery

See yourself as a sport star in the field you are interested in. Use the screen technique. There are over six hundred muscle complexes covering the two hundred bones in your body. Picture these muscles contract and relax to strengthen your power. It helps in physical achievements to exaggerate your skill.

Suggestion

"Every time I play, or practice, I will exceed my previous performance. I am physically, mentally and emotionally ready to reach the top."

STRESS MANAGMENT...

Becoming stress-free and maintaining a calm perspective, begins with a new attitude. Many ailments have their origin in accumulated mental and physical tension.

Imagery

After getting into a comfortable position, take a few deep breaths and close your eyes. Shift your mind to your feet. Think of your toes as bubbles, separated from the rest of your feet. Let them float away in your reverie. Think of the rest of your feet as very soft, light, and airy, like balloons. Focus on your ankles as loose, limp and disjointed, just dangling. As you affirm this mental image, you let your mind wander upward to your calf muscles. Think calf muscles as heavy; knees loose, limp, and disjointed. Think of your hips loose, limp, and disjointed, your buttocks sinking into the surface supporting you. You are now relaxed from the tip of your toes up to the center of your body. Now start at the top of your head and work down to your navel. Breath slowly and deeply throughout the imagery.

Suggestion

"I will slow down and take it easy. Nothing is so serious as to make me feel pressured or stressed out."

STROKE VICTIMS...

Hypnosis combined with physical therapy, shows the most promise of bringing about improvements. A common side effect of stroke is slurred speech or loss of control over the larynx. Some other ways that hypnosis has helped stroke victims include: Facial paralysis. Hearing impairment. Loss of muscle strength, etc.

Imagery

The best visualization is to go back in time to a happy, healthy day before the stroke happened. See yourself, walking running, speaking normally.

Suggestion

"I have high expectations of returning to my normal self. I will follow my doctor's advice, improve with physical therapy, and a positive mental attitude."

STUDY HABITS...

If you enjoy learning, you will tend to accomplish more, than if your attitude is negative. We live in a world where the under-educated are often unemployable. To avoid poverty, we need knowledge. Using Self-hypnosis in the lightest stage (relaxation and concentration) the mind becomes more retentive.

Imagery

See the advantages of an education to earn a better salary. Imagine you are in an employment office. Watching the process of being interviewed. One applicant without education is turned away. You sit down and answer questions with ease and you are hired.

Suggestion

"I will take advantage of every opportunity to learn and improve myself. I will practice self-hypnosis to improve my memory and study habits."

STUTTERING...

The fear of speaking keeps many people from expressing themselves. Stuttering does not have to be permanent. The younger the stuttering, the least difficult is the correction, because it is not a deeply ingrained in the autonomic reflexes. Adults can also be helped, but the process takes longer.

Imagery

The best results can be obtained by rehearsing a situations where the subject is with people who trigger discomfort. The subject communicates by whispering or singing. People who stutter, have better control when they alter the kind of sound they project. See yourself in front of a mirror, speaking one word at a time, and pronouncing that word very slowly. Another helpful vision is to superimpose your face onto another person, who does not stutter. The alteration can trick the vocal reflexes to emulate the selected person.

Suggestion
"I will not rush to respond to people, but instead, I will relax, take a breath and think before I speak."

SUCCESS...
You can't become a shining star, if you cast a cloud over your own brilliance. People often make "predictions" about what they can and cannot do. When you tell yourself that you can't make it, the orders are accepted and carried out. Here are five requirements for true success:

1...Physical health with a high level energy
2...Passionate desire to change for the better
3...An overall love of people, built on trust
4...Selecting worthy goals, short and long-term
5...Peace of mind, based on self-appreciation

Imagery
See success in your future. Strolling along on a beautiful day, you see a movie house with your name on the marquee. You go in and sit down and watch the screen. You are the viewer, the star, the director and producer.

Suggestion
"I have everything that it takes to fulfill my life. I have no trouble getting cooperation from others, when I need it. I will reach my maximum capacity."

SUICIDE...
This is the eighth cause of death among humans and the third affecting youth. Over half of the elderly die, due to suicide. Hypnosis helps as intervention and prevention, whenever possible.

Imagery
Because hopelessness, is the first sign of depression, visualization needs to

bring high hopes for something special happening. Imagine yourself at a meeting of the "Optimists of the World." You are giving a talk on how to overcome pessimism. See yourself rewarded and applauded.

Suggestion

"I have an optimistic point of view about all events in my life. The problems were learning experiences. In all future situations I will remember that I have the power to overcome and move forward."

SURGERY- POST-OP...

After surgery, the recovering time can be dramatically reduced by using the method described here. Zero into the area of healing. This will send added energy and endorphins (mind chemicals) to accelerate the natural ability, inherent in you.

Imagery

The recovery period after illness or accident can be made more pleasant and healing can be accelerated greatly by entering a trance level of any depth that is comfortable for the patient

Suggestion

"I will fall asleep each night in comfort, and heal myself all through the night. Each morning I will awaken with great energy and feel better and better."

SWEATING PROFUSELY...

First, check whether the condition is dietary. Overweight and over-salting your food can contribute to the perspiration distress.

Imagery

Challenge your subconscious mind to reveal the cause of your sweating problem. Picture the "magic mirror on the wall" that will tell you all. Project the question: "Why do I sweat too much?" Wait for the answer. It will appear. Ask another question: "How can I correct the problem?" The answer will appear.

Suggestion

"I stay cool, calm and confident under all conditions. I will keep my breathing pattern deep and smooth, and think things through to avoid feeling nervous.

TEEN PREGNANCY...

When a boy and girl reach their adolescence, they usually are not ready for the responsibility of marriage. but they are biologically ready for sexual intimacy and reproducing babies. If teenage females are sexually active they must insist on contraception. The United States has the highest teen pregnancy of any industrial nation.

Imagery

The most preventive visualization is aversion therapy. This consists in the young woman seeing a preview of herself, in full pregnancy and mentally experiencing how giving birth would look, feel and change her life.

Suggestion

"I am contented to wait for a more responsible time and a lasting relationship, so the child can have a normal upbringing."

TENNIS...

Many professionals practice what they call "mental tennis." Which is actually a form of focused concentration on the hypnoidal level with eyes open, when you actually play on the court. However, eyes are closed when you rehearse under self-hypnosis.

Imagery

See yourself balanced and poised, holding your racket in a position to return your opponent's serve. Keep your eye on the ball. As it reaches you, see where you want it to go and connect with super-power. Picture yourself as the winner at the end of the game.

Suggestion

"I am putting my mind power into the game. Every time I enter the hypnotic trance, I will see improvement and transfer it onto the tennis court."

TRICHOTILLOMANIA

(Hair Pulling)... This compulsive habit usually starts with pulling eyelashes, eyebrows and eventually may escalate to removing all hair from the head and body. It has been diagnosed as a psychiatric disorder affecting five to twenty million people, mainly females. Like any obsessiveness, improvement is possible with self-hypnosis, after being trained by a professional hypnotist.

Imagery
After reaching the altered state, pinpoint your imagination to concentrate on the particular area you wish to protect against the compulsive behavior. In this case, concentrate on the scalp. Picture the hair roots under the scalp. See the roots as twice as strong and twice as large as you would normally think of them. See them as resistant warriors who do not wish to be disturbed.

Suggestion
"Every time my subconscious mind sends an impulse to pull out hair from anywhere on my face, head or body, my conscious mind will immediately stop the action."

TERMINAL ILLNESS...
Blissful imagery while in an altered state of mind, can prepare the incurable and elderly, to die in a calm state of peacefulness, because it helps them discover peace of mind and spirituality.

Imagery
The induction is standard, with progressive relaxation directed to the most troublesome physical part of the body. Then the tunnel of spiritual light with music and laughter and the greeting of friends, departed. There are loving arms waiting to embrace and caress.

Suggestion
"I am at peace with myself. I have transcended all earthly cares and anxieties. I feel uplifted, protected and directed by higher spiritual forces, which surround and comfort me."

TIME MANAGMENT...
For a fruitful life have a "Time Plan." Plan your life and live your plan. Make each day count by, using time for accomplishments. In this way you stop wasting time worrying about the past or the future and instead make each present moment count.

Imagery

You are facing a wall chart, which shows each hour. At the top of the chart, indicate what you will accomplish that day. Now you fill in the blanks hour by hour, to indicate what you will be accomplishing during each time slot. This is your way to structure your time to the best advantage.

Suggestion

"I will enjoy making the most out of my time. Every day in every way, I will accomplish more and more."

TINNITUS RELIEF...

Emotional factors are often associated with this condition, also called Meniere's disease. There are as many as fifty million American sufferers. They report that stress situations accentuate the symptoms, such as ringing in the ears, whistling or buzzing sounds in the head.

Imagery

After basic progressive relaxation and induction to the altered state of mind is accomplished, differential relaxation aimed at neck, back of head and nerves surrounding the ears. Visualize the affected area and visualize the exhalation of each breath through the problem area. See the muscles surrounding the jaw and head become loosely unraveled.

Suggestion

This condition requires that suggestion be given by a professional. Post-hypnotic suggestion should be used by the practitioner, as follows: Ask the person to describe the kind of sound he/she hears. Through word association, search for a clue, a person, place or situation to connect the sound to. This will help determine the wording of corrective suggestion. An audio tape to support the therapy works very well.

TOILET TRAINING...

Even toddlers respond to positive suggestion, especially at bedtime. This is when they tend to drift into the alpha-theta trance level due to normal sleepiness.

Imagery

The parent sits down on the child's bed and holds his/her hand and speaks the suggestions softly, and with unconditional love.

Suggestion

"Today was a very good day. I really enjoyed being with you. You're doing really well and tomorrow will be even better. Every day you grow a little bigger and do the right things."

TOURETTE SYNDROME...

This disorder is more common than most people think. It can take on various forms: Motor tics, such as involuntary movements. Facial twitching. Uncontrolled shouting (sometimes obscenities). Vocal tics can also include barking, grunting, and sneezing. The problem affects more boys than girls and begins at about seven years old. Group hypnosis has proved helpful, because the children try to outdo each other in the degree of their progress.

Imagery

This is not a simple problem for self-hypnosis training, but requires a skilled hypnosis therapist with psychological training. Progressive relaxation is the first step, followed by directed imagery of the condition taking a vaporous form and blown away by the child's forceful breathing.

Suggestion

"Every day, in every way, I have more power over what I do. I can decide to act normal and feel happy."

TRANSEXUAL GENDER IDENTITY...

Hypnosis is a valuable tool to help those who decide to alter their gender. This works equally well for post surgery patients as well as transvestites who choose to keep their sex organs intact. You can become what you want to be by first picturing the changes.

Imagery

You can use either the mirror, or the mental-movie techniques. See the changes in the way you dress, walk, talk and move your body. Picture yourself at a social gathering, where you are totally accepted as living normally in the gender roll you have chosen.

Suggestion

"I am emotionally, and physically capable of making the changeover without anxiety or regrets."

UNDERACHIEVERS...

This applies to well over half the youthful population regardless of ethnic or racial background. Raising consciousness and motivation by uncovering hidden abilities. This spurs one's desire to increase achievements. This type of person is best served in a community setting where people can communicate with each other and lend a helping hand.

Imagery

Picture yourself doing something you really do well and are proud of. You are being praised for your effort and encouraged to do more. Taking action will put you in the driver's seat, rather than feel like a wounded passenger, under other people's direction.

Suggestion

"My confidence is growing with every step I take in the right direction. I am building my self-esteem and receiving respect from others."

VIBRATIONS TO ATTRACT...

Good vibrations are a sign of well-being. They are bad when we sense the other's tension and lack of confidence. Positive vibrations have opposite results and are contagious. They reverberate from the CORE of another person's state of mind. At best, there is a glow of magnetic radiance all around you.

Imagery

Picture the ocean's waves in perpetual motion. The rolling sea breaks its ripples onto the shore and changes the look of the sand. Think of the rhythm of time — a day is born, and drifts into noon, then sunset and darkness. The cycle repeats again and again. The breeze rustles the trees and sways its branches, which sets each leaf into vibrations of its own.

Much of this continuous interaction goes on unnoticed. Still every tremble leaves its mark.

Suggestion

"I will relax with the rhythms of nature. I sway freely like a willow tree, and move with events. I am flexible and easy to get along with."

VIBRATOR DEPENDENCY...

Millions of women buy and use sexual vibrators to stimulate themselves to the point of orgasm. However, a sensory dependency problem has developed which is interfering with their ability to respond to normal coitus with a male partner. This is easily corrected with self-hypnosis which can be used before self-masturbation as well as during coitus.

Imagery

Picture yourself with a partner, even when you are alone with your vibrator. Visualize yourself being made love to passionately. Transfer the feeling of the vibrator (or you can use the actual vibrator) in the shared experience.

Suggestion

"I will be able to reach a climax with or without the vibrator. I am not dependent on any mechanical device. Human intimacy makes me feel much better."

VIOLENT BEHAVIOR...

Violence is learned behavior, and as such, can be unlearned. Babies are not born violent; they can be trained to be non-combative, rather than confrontational. Violent people blame others for their emotional distress. However, it never helps resolve the conflict because blaming others keeps you a victim of your own inner turmoil. We must reverse degeneration to regeneration and by so doing enable the human spirit.

Imagery

Before you lose control, you will see a STOP sign in your right brain that slows down the emotion. If you feel the heat rising, an alarm will sound. Imagine the red STOP light flashing, in your mind.

Suggestion

"My wise subconscious will signal me, and I will obey the image of the STOP sign. I will think of wiser, alternative behavior."

VOICE TRAINING...

Actors, singers and politicians often use hypnosis to improve the quality of their voices and to protect themselves against strain. Some people have chronic problems with laryngitis and inability to speak with clarity.

Imagery

Start with the mirror technique. Visualize yourself looking confident. Listen to yourself with a third ear, as a bystander. You project with resonance, clarity and power.

Suggestion

"I have everything I need to improve my voice delivering. I will transform my life by improving the way I sound. Day by day, it gets better and better."

VOYEURISM

(Peeping Tom)... This is an uncontrollable obsessive desire to see people in an intimate way, without being seen by them. Because this is an intrusion of one's privacy, it is against the law. This is a problem which is found mostly among men.

Imagery

The corrective vision during hypnotic meditation, is an aversion technique, in which the roles are reversed: The voyeur is now at the mercy of a vicious-looking Peeping Tom. The subject imagines himself in a personal situation, such as going to the bathroom, or having sex. Suddenly, he is startled by an angry face peering in through a window.

Suggestion

"I will respect other people's privacy and will never again invade their territory. If the urge presents itself to me, instead of following through, a red light will flash on a sign that says: STOP! NO TRESPASSING ALLOWED!

WARTS...

In many cases, warts appear as stigmata (mental markings) in areas where previous trauma took place. This is especially true of genital warts. Instances of anal and vagina warts may be the result of forced entry, and subsequent irritation of genital tissue. There is a psychological component to the problem, because it may become a symbol to recall insult to the body.

Imagery

Seeing the affected area as clear and normal provides a vision for the corrective area of the brain to follow. Visualize the diminishing in size. It also helps to think back (with age regression technique) to the area before the problem manifested itself.

Suggestion

"The warts have been shrinking with every breath. Now they are gone and will never come back. They serve no purpose and I don't want them."

WEIGHT LOSS...

Are you overweight? Over eighty million Americans are. An excess of even five to ten pounds can cut down on your stamina and self-esteem. Exploring the causes that lead more than twenty-five percent of all Americans to obesity reveals the fact that fat is often a cover for something deeper. It usually has an emotional base.

Imagery.

Picture yourself standing in front of a full length three way mirror. See yourself front view, back view and side view. Make all of the changes that you want for yourself. Slimmer here, firmer there. Notice a calendar on the wall see the goal-date that you have set for reaching your best weight and improved image. Now get on a scale and weigh yourself. Notice that you have reached your goal. Imagine yourself as a clothes model modeling clothes in the size that you prefer. The audience applauds your success.

Suggestion

"With every breath I am full and satisfied without extra calories. I will follow the five point program for staying slim permanently. I will:

1. Postpone eating sometime;
2. Choose low calorie foods;
3. Chew all food very slowly;
4. Breath deeply to metabolize;
5. Exercise routinely, daily."

WHEELCHAIR BOUND...

Hypnosis can enable the disabled to discover their aptitudes and learn skills which will optimize their innate talents. Also, if they are in the process of recovery or healing, hypnosis can be helpful in speeding up the progress.

Imagery

Visualize the television or movie screen with your name on it. You are the performer, the director and the writer of this drama.

Suggestion

"I will optimize my abilities and become stronger and stronger, day by day."

WOUND HEALING...

Hypnotic imagery with focused suggestions can cut healing time greatly. This is a case where the deeper you go the sooner the results will show, so each time you enter trance use deepening techniques — counting down, and elevator descending.

Imagery

Picture the area of the wound and see the skin and flesh surrounding the wound disappear until only the wound is visible. Next zero in your differential focus to the edges of the wound and picture the skin drawing together. Then see the wound gone entirely.

Suggestion

"Every time I enter my healing center, I can free myself of any imperfection. I will do everything necessary not to get hurt, but if I do, I will repair the damage quickly and easily.

WRITER'S BLOCK....

Hypnosis is a cognitive way of by-passing blocks stuck in your psyche. It helps you "seize the moment" in a state of NOW. Goals are clarified and anxieties cease to exist.

Imagery

In a light to medium trance, picture yourself seated at your computer. See a title on your screen. Now, focus on your fingers typing on the keyboard. See the words and sentences, rapidly appearing on your screen, as if you are being directed by a higher power.

Suggestion

"The block is gone and will not return. Creative thoughts are flowing freely. No future problems."

XENOPHOBIA...

This fear of strangers and foreigners can escalate to an obsessive compulsion. This limits the afflicted person in areas of work and social interactions. This person also gives the impression to others of being limited in intelligence.

Imagery

Picture yourself at a happy celebration. The people are warm and friendly. They are of all races and colors. They surround you to admire and complement you on your personal achievements.

Suggestion

"Each time I meet a new person, I am more comfortable. I smile and act pleasant and they return my good mood. I enjoy learning new things from people who seem to be different than me."

YOUTHFULNESS...

Neglecting health not only invites aging, but the undertaker as well. Fortunately, it is never too late to reverse the process. Because attitude affect activity, thinking young, retards aging. Hypnosis increases energy, whether you decide to run a marathon or just stay in bed and make love.

Imagery

This calls for the "Age Regression" technique, using the magic mirror. When you see yourself behaving with youthful energy, you trick your mind into believing you are capable of doing thingsas you did, years ago.

Suggestion

"I think young. I talk young. I look young. I behave young. Time can only enhance my qualities. I do not grow older, I grow better."

ZEST...

This is emotion put into motion. Passion combined with action brings results. Socrates said, "The years wrinkle our skin, but lack of enthusiasm wrinkles our soul." Zest makes you feel your best.

Imagery

Picture yourself leading a parade of energetic marchers. You are going to set free all the problems of the world. This mission will make you totally joyful and free from all previous limitations.

Suggestion

Imagine yourself shouting out: "Yes, I can! I can, and I will get where I need to go. I am overflowing with energy and passion and others will follow."

ZOOPHOBIA...

This is an unreal terror of animals, even those that are tame and domesticated. Zoophobia usually stems from an early childhood experience of being frightened by an animal over which the subject had no control.

Imagery

See yourself as an animal trainer, working in a circus where you tame lions and tigers. They do exactly as you tell them to. Next picture an animal you are afraid of as a child and see the emotions reversed. The animal is afraid of you. Next picture the human and the animal developing trust and becoming friends.

Suggestion

"I do not fear any kind of animal, because I have greater intelligence. My thinking brain guides me to become invincible. I will act with confidence, because of this natural power."